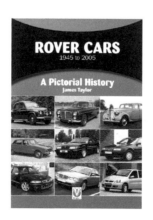

ROVER CARS
1945 to 2005

A Pictorial History
James Taylor

Also in the Pictorial History series:
Austin Cars, 1948 to 1990 (Rowe)
Rootes Cars of the 50s, 60s & 70s – Hillman, Humber, Singer, Sunbeam & Talbot (Rowe)
Triumph & Standard Cars, 1945 to 1984 (Warrington)
Wolseley Cars, 1948 to 1975 (Rowe)

More from Veloce:

Essential Buyer's Guide series
Land Rover Discovery Series 1 (1989-1998) (Taylor)
Land Rover Discovery Series 2 (1998-2004) (Taylor)
Land Rover Series I, II & IIA (Thurman)
Land Rover Series III (Thurman)
Range Rover – First Generation models 1970 to 1996 (Taylor)
Range Rover – Second Generation 1994-2001 (Taylor)
Range Rover – Third Generation L322 (2002-2012) (Taylor)
Rover 2000, 2200 & 3500 (Marrocco)

Those Were The Days ... Series
Austerity Motoring (Bobbitt)
Austins, The last real (Peck)
British and European Trucks of the 1970s (Peck)
British Lorries of the 1950s (Bobbitt)
British Lorries of the 1960s (Bobbitt)
British Touring Car Racing (Collins)
British Police Cars (Walker)
British Woodies (Peck)
Don Hayter's MGB Story – The birth of the MGB in MG's Abingdon Design & Development Office (Hayter)
Endurance Racing at Silverstone in the 1970s & 1980s (Parker)
Hot Rod & Stock Car Racing in Britain in the 1980s (Neil)
MG's Abingdon Factory (Moylan)
Motor Racing at Brands Hatch in the Seventies (Parker)
Motor Racing at Brands Hatch in the Eighties (Parker)
Motor Racing at Crystal Palace (Collins)
Motor Racing at Goodwood in the Sixties (Gardiner)
Motor Racing at Oulton Park in the 1960s (McFadyen)
Motor Racing at Oulton Park in the 1970s (McFadyen)
Motor Racing at Thruxton in the 1970s (Grant-Braham)
Motor Racing at Thruxton in the 1980s (Grant-Braham)
Superprix – The Story of Birmingham Motor Race (Page & Collins)
Three Wheelers (Bobbitt)

General
Alfa Romeo Giulia Coupé GT & GTA (Tipler)
Alfa Romeo Montreal – The dream car that came true (Taylor)
Alfa Romeo Montreal – The Essential Companion (Taylor)
Alfa Tipo 33 (McDonough & Collins)
An Austin Anthology (Stringer)
An Austin Anthology II (Stringer)
An English Car Designer Abroad (Birtwhistle)

An Incredible Journey (Falls & Reisch)
Anatomy of the Classic Mini (Huthert & Ely)
Anatomy of the Works Minis (Moylan)
Armstrong-Siddeley (Smith)
Art Deco and British Car Design (Down)
Autodrome (Collins & Ireland)
Automotive A-Z, Lane's Dictionary of Automotive Terms (Lane)
Automotive Mascots (Kay & Springate)
Bentley Continental, Corniche and Azure (Bennett)
Bentley MkVI, Rolls-Royce Silver Wraith, Dawn & Cloud/Bentley R & S-Series (Nutland)
Bluebird CN7 (Stevens)
BMC Competitions Department Secrets (Turner, Chambers & Browning)
British at Indianapolis, The (Wagstaff)
British Cars, The Complete Catalogue of, 1895-1975 (Culshaw & Horrobin)
BRM – A Mechanic's Tale (Salmon)
Caravan, Improve & Modify Your (Porter)
Caravans, The Illustrated History 1919-1959 (Jenkinson)
Caravans, The Illustrated History From 1960 (Jenkinson)
Car-tastrophes – 80 automotive atrocities from the past 20 years (Honest John, Fowler)Classic British Car Electrical Systems (Astley)
Cortina – Ford's Bestseller (Robson)
Cosworth – The Search for Power (6th edition) (Robson)
Coventry Climax Racing Engines (Hammill)
Dorset from the Sea – The Jurassic Coast from Lyme Regis to Old Harry Rocks photographed from its best viewpoint (also Souvenir Edition) (Belasco)
Draw & Paint Cars – How to (Gardiner)
Drive on the Wild Side, A – 20 Extreme Driving Adventures From Around the World (Weaver)
Driven – An Elegy to Cars, Roads & Motorsport (Aston)
Essential Guide to Driving in Europe, The (Parish)
Fate of the Sleeping Beauties, The (op de Weegh/ Hottendorff/op de Weegh)
France: the essential guide for car enthusiasts – 200 things for the car enthusiast to see and do (Parish)
The Good, the Mad and the Ugly ... not to mention Jeremy Clarkson (Dron)
Immortal Austin Seven (Morgan)
India - The Shimmering Dream (Reisch/Falls (translator))
Inside the Rolls-Royce & Bentley Styling Department – 1971 to 2001 (Hull)
Jaguar - All the Cars (4th Edition) (Thorley)
Jaguar from the shop floor (Martin)
Jaguar E-type Factory and Private Competition Cars (Griffiths)
Jaguar, The Rise of (Price)
Jaguar XJ 220 – The Inside Story (Moreton)
Jaguar XJ-S, The Book of the (Long)
The Jowett Jupiter – The car that leaped to fame (Nankivell)
Karmann-Ghia Coupé & Convertible (Bobbitt)
Land Rover Design - 70 years of success (Hull)
Land Rover Emergency Vehicles (Taylor)
Land Rover Series III Reborn (Porter)
Land Rover, The Half-ton Military (Cook)
Land Rovers in British Military Service – coil sprung models 1970 to 2007 (Taylor)
Lotus 18 Colin Chapman's U-turn (Whitelock)
Lotus 49 (Oliver)
Lotus Elan and Plus 2 Source Book (Vale)

Making a Morgan (Hensing)
Marketingmobiles, The Wonderful Wacky World of (Hale)
Maximum Mini (Booij)
Meet the English (Bowie)
MG, Made in Abingdon (Frampton)
MGA (Price Williams)
MGB & MGB GT– Expert Guide (Auto-doc Series) (Williams)
MGB Electrical Systems Updated & Revised Edition (Astley)
MGB – The Illustrated History, Updated Fourth Edition (Wood & Burrell)
The MGC GTS Lightweights (Morys)
Micro Caravans (Jenkinson)
Mini Cooper – The Real Thing! (Tipler)
Mini Minor to Asia Minor (West)
Morgan Maverick (Lawrence)
Morgan 3 Wheeler – back to the future!, The (Dron)
Morris Minor, 70 Years on the Road (Newell)
Motor Movies – The Posters! (Veysey)
Motorhomes, The Illustrated History (Jenkinson)
Motorsport In colour, 1950s (Wainwright)
Nothing Runs – Misadventures in the Classic, Collectable & Exotic Car Biz (Slutsky)
Racing Colours – Motor Racing Compositions 1908-2009 (Newman)
Renewable Energy Home Handbook, The (Porter)
Roads with a View – England's greatest views and how to find them by road (Corfield)
Rolls-Royce Silver Shadow/Bentley T Series Corniche & Camargue – Revised & Enlarged Edition (Bobbitt)
Rolls-Royce Silver Spirit, Silver Spur & Bentley Mulsanne 2nd Edition (Bobbitt)
Rover P4 (Bobbitt)
Schlumpf – The intrigue behind the most beautiful car collection in the world (Op de Weegh & Op de Weegh)
Singer Story: Cars, Commercial Vehicles, Bicycles & Motorcycle (Atkinson)
Sprite Caravans, The Story of (Jenkinson)
Standard Motor Company, The Book of the (Robson)
Tales from the Toolbox (Oliver)
Tatra – The Legacy of Hans Ledwinka, Updated & Enlarged Collector's Edition of 1500 copies (Margolius & Henry)
Taxi! The Story of the 'London' Taxicab (Bobbitt)
This Day in Automotive History (Corey)
To Boldly Go – twenty six vehicle designs that dared to be different (Hull)
Triumph Cars – The Complete Story (new 3rd edition) (Robson)
Triumph TR6 (Kimberley)
Volkswagen Bus or Van to Camper, How to Convert (Porter)
VW Bus – 40 Years of Splitties, Bays & Wedges (Copping)
VW T5 Camper Conversion Manual (Porter)
VW Campers (Copping)
You & Your Jaguar XK8/XKR – Buying, Enjoying, Maintaining, Modifying – New Edition (Thorley)
Which Oil? – Choosing the right oils & greases for your antique, vintage, veteran, classic or collector car (Michell)
Works MGs, The (Allison & Browning)
Works Minis, The Last (Purves & Brenchley)
Works Rally Mechanic (Moylan)

www.veloce.co.uk

First published in September 2018, and reprinted October 2019 by Veloce Publishing Limited, Veloce House, Parkway Farm Business Park, Middle Farm Way, Poundbury, Dorchester DT1 3AR, England. Tel +44 (0)1305 260068 / Fax 01305 250479 / e-mail info@veloce.co.uk / web www.veloce.co.uk or www.velocebooks.com.
ISBN: 978-1-787116-09-2 / UPC: 6-36847-01609-8

ROVER CARS
1945 to 2005

A Pictorial History
James Taylor

VELOCE

CONTENTS

Sixty years of Rover cars. 6
M Model 11
P2 12
P3 14
P4 15
P5, P5B 20
P6, P6B 23
P6BS and P9 26
P7 29
P8 30
SD1 31
Australian Quintet 34
200, first series 35
800 (1986-98) 37
Australian 416i 39
200, second series 41
200 Cabriolet 44
200 'Tomcat' 46

400, first series (1990-1995) 48
400 Tourer (1994-1998) 49
Rover Metro and 100 (1990-1997) 50
600 (1993-1998) 52
400, second series (1995-1999) 56
200, third series (1995-1999) 59
75 (1998-2005) 62
25 (1999-2005) 65
45 (1999-2005) 66
Streetwise (2003-2005) 68
CityRover (2003-2005) 70
The non-Rovers (1986-2000) 71
    Mini (1987-2000) .71
    Metro (1987-90) .72
    Maestro (1987-92) 72
    Montego (1987-1995) 73
Gas turbines 74
Index 80

Sixty years of Rover cars

The Rover Company emerged from the 1939-1945 war in a strong position. On behalf of the Air Ministry (Ministry of Aircraft Production), Rover had managed two of the 'shadow' factories that had helped ensure production of military aircraft during the hostilities, and was now given the option of purchasing one of these at Solihull, south-east of Birmingham. The site was a large one, but Rover prudently bought some of the farmland around it as well, to allow for eventual expansion. Meanwhile, its former premises in Coventry, destroyed during the Blitz in 1940, were sold on.

At this stage, Rover was a well-respected independent motor manufacturer, known for its well-engineered, well-built cars of discreet appearance, that appealed to the British professional classes. The company would remain so for another two decades before joining The Leyland Group, to protect itself against mergers and buy-outs elsewhere in the industry that seemed likely to threaten its continued existence. It would also continue to see itself as primarily a builder of cars – 'One of Britain's Fine Cars' was a 1940s slogan – even though the truth was that it had become primarily

a builder of light commercial vehicles. The Land Rover, introduced in 1948 to provide a high-volume export product, had quickly exceeded car production by a wide margin, and certainly accounted for Rover's survival as an independent car maker for so long.

The Rovers of the 1940s, '50s and '60s were all prestigious cars. They had an excellent build quality and were thoughtfully engineered, with discreet styling that did not date quickly. The models of this period were the P2 and P3, with their essentially pre-war styling, the much-loved 'Auntie' P4, the elegant and slightly imperious P5, and the technically advanced P6.

Rover-British Leyland

Under Leyland from 1967, (later 'British Leyland' – when there were further mergers in 1968) Rover initially retained its independence. By 1969, it was clear that there were model clashes within the British Leyland empire, and within two years, Rover had been denied the funds to go ahead with two planned designs. The company's engineers

The basic style of the Viking ship emblem was retained for the metal badge used on the P3 models, in this case, a 75.

The first P4s, in 1949, had this unique version of the Viking ship emblem. It was on the nose of the bonnet rather than on the grille.

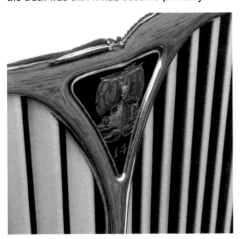

Rover had used a Viking ship emblem, in various forms, since long before the war. When production got under way in the second half of the 1940s, the pre-war type of enamelled metal badge was revived. This is on a Rover 14.

were obliged to work with their counterparts at Triumph on a third new model, and in 1972, Rover and Triumph were formally merged, becoming part of British Leyland's Specialist Division. Although many of the old Rover engineers and designers remained in place, Rover as a separate company had ceased to exist.

Somehow – and perhaps it was the world-wide acknowledgement of the Land Rover sub-brand that helped – Rover survived as a concept. Although there was a move to brand all models as Leyland types after British Leyland ran out of money and entered government ownership in 1974, and, despite the appalling quality that afflicted most British Leyland brands in the 1970s, the Rover name still stood for cars of distinction and quality.

The Rover P5B and P6 range were still in production during the early days of British Leyland, and the P6 was replaced by the SD1 in 1976.

The Honda alliance

After a further re-organisation in 1981, the Rover brand was again retained and pushed to the fore. Under the newly created Austin Rover division, there were still cars that were badged as Rovers, even though from 1982 they were no longer made at the Solihull factory, which was given over entirely to Land Rover manufacture. Instead, they were made at the old Morris

plant in Cowley and, later, the Austin plant at Longbridge.

This was the period when British Leyland had entered an alliance with Honda in Japan, and the new Rovers of the 1980s and early 1990s would be designed in collaboration with that company. The first and second series 200, the 800, and first-series 400 were all fruits of this collaboration in the 1980s. And in the first half of the 1990s, the Rover 600 was yet another jointly designed model. Yet all these cars had been Anglicised enough to retain the aura of quality and luxury that had distinguished the traditional products of the old Rover Company.

In Australia, a Honda model was re-badged and sold as a Rover Quintet even before the first Honda alliance cars were released in Britain. A second model with a similar provenance would follow in the mid-1980s, as the Rover 416i.

Austin inheritance

Yet another re-organisation followed in 1986, when what was left of British Leyland was renamed as The Rover Group, allegedly because the Rover name was the only one of those available to British Leyland that still retained some credibility.

This re-organisation left some older British Leyland models, originally badged as Austins, out on a limb. Although they continued to be built in Rover Group factories, they were not Rovers,

This metal version of the badge was used from early 1952.

In the late 1950s, plastic badges were introduced. This one is on a P4 105S from 1958.

and the company realised that they would not be accepted as such in the short term; so when the Austin name was formally abandoned in late 1987, these orphaned models – Metro, Maestro, Montego and Mini – were simply known by their model-names. Only the Metro would later become a full Rover, although the Montego did wear Rover badges in some export territories.

in the 1960s, not all the grille badges carried the model name. On this early 1960s P5 model, the Rover 3-litre name is carried separately from the Viking ship emblem.

This stylised version of the Viking ship was used on the P5 and P5B Coupés. Originally drawn for the Rover apprentices' headed notepaper (according to legend), it became reversed when transferred to the cars, which is why the flag at the masthead is pointing left rather than right!

New wave

Few buyers cared that the Rovers of the 1980s and 1990s were Honda designs. Most still recognised that the Rover name stood for some quintessentially British qualities, including high-quality appointments and what has since become known in the motor industry as 'premium' appeal.

Behind the scenes, though, it was undeniable that Rover had changed almost beyond all recognition. The last Rover was built at the company's old Solihull factory in 1981, and that factory was then turned over entirely to Land Rover manufacture. Many of the old Rover engineers and designers had gone by now, so the name was really a memory of earlier greatness, and the methods by which the cars were designed and developed

For the P6, a new and larger grille badge was introduced, with the Rover name and gold highlights.

This 'gilded' version of the Viking ship was only ever used on the P5B models.

had changed radically. Instead of being the brainchild of a few key engineers, each one was now designed and developed by a much larger group of people.

In 1989, The Rover Group was sold out of government ownership to British Aerospace, who largely performed a caretaking function for five years. Yet The Rover Group had begun to grow stronger again. Its renaissance had begun with the advanced K-series engine in 1989, and this was followed by new car designs such as the R3 200 series, and the superb new 75. The 25 and 45 were face-lifts of existing designs, but gave a welcome new freshness to the marque as the new century began.

In the meantime, British Aerospace had sold Rover to the German BMW Group in 1994, and this promised great things as BMW improved working practices and encouraged new designs. But improvements in profits remained elusive, and by 2000, the Germans had had enough. In May that year, The Rover Group was sold to a consortium called The Phoenix Group; Land Rover, meanwhile, was in a much healthier position and was sold to Ford.

MG Rover

A revival of the MG marque had already been planned, and the company was renamed MG Rover Group Ltd in September 2000. It launched into the new century with optimism, developing MG variants of its Rover models to appeal to a wider customer base, but a desperate shortage of cash reduced its ability to develop genuinely new models. The Streetwise, based on the 25, was a bizarre attempt to get more out of an existing design.

As for a small car, the lack of funds obliged Rover to buy in an outsourced design, and the CityRover of 2003 really did not live up to customer expectations of the brand.

Attempts to forge new alliances with other manufacturers, particularly in China, all failed to produce the necessary funds in time, and in 2005, MG Rover collapsed. Its remains were sold to some of the Chinese companies with which it had been in negotiation, and the Rover name ceased to exist.

This clever skeletal interpretation of the Rover badge was designed in the early 1970s, and appeared on early SD1 models. It was not much liked, and was replaced by a more recognisable Viking ship badge after a few years.

This was the later SD1 nose badge, now in colour, as well as incorporating the Rover name.

The Rover 800, first series 200 and 400, and the 600 all had this amended version of the grille badge.

An anomaly: this is the Viking ship emblem on the Australian-market Rover Quintet, specially designed to fill the space originally intended for a Honda badge.

The Rover 75 introduced in 1998 retained the essential features of the Viking ship badge, which was adapted for other models. This is it, on a Rover 25.

The Rover badge was re-styled in late 2003 to give a more modern look, but the essentials of the Viking ship were still readily recognisable.

M Model

The story of how Rover planned to introduce a 'baby' car after the Second World War is well known. Its thinking was that in the difficult economic times that would certainly follow the war, buyers would want small and economical models. However, that was not what they wanted at all; they wanted bigger cars that would help them feel that better times had arrived, so Rover abandoned plans for what it called the M Model (M, presumably, for miniature).

The M Model was unquestionably inspired by the pre-war Fiat 500. Design work began in 1944, and there were multiple iterations of the car's styling in 1945-1946. A special

699cc derivative of Rover's new IOE engine, designed before the war by the company's engines man, Jack Swaine, was also drawn up. This was expected to put out 28.5hp at 5000rpm, which, in tandem with the lightweight all-alloy platform-like chassis, was to give the car performance similar to that of a pre-war Rover 12.

Prototypes were ready before the end of 1946, and, according to legend, there were six of them – although that may be an exaggeration. One was tested by The Motor in 1949, by which time the project had long been abandoned. Unfortunately, none have survived, although one was in daily use by a member of the Rover engineering staff until the late 1950s or early 1960s.

The proposed M Model had a lot in common with the Fiat 500, its wheelbase being almost the same size. There were coil springs on all four wheels, and rear-wheel drive. The car was intended as a two-seater.

The 699cc four-cylinder engine was mounted ahead of the front wheels, and had the same IOE architecture as Rover's planned new post-war engines.

P2 10hp, 12hp, 14hp and 16hp (1945-1947)

Although Rover had been thinking about its post-war models for some time before the war actually ended, the company was far from ready to start making anything new when it received the green light to build cars again during 1945. The best it could do was what other British car makers were also doing, and that was to put its most recent pre-war models back into production, with minimal changes. One of the changes was to offer models with left-hand-drive for the very first time.

Most of those immediate pre-war models

had entered production in autumn 1936, as 1937 models, and they had been very well-received by the professional classes, who were Rover's primary customers, so although they looked old-fashioned by global standards in 1945 (and those standards were conditioned by American designs), their target buyers actually appreciated their discreet conservatism. Unfortunately, as Rover discovered, they were less well-received in export markets.

Rover established production lines for these cars at its new Solihull factory, probably using some tooling salvaged from its bombed Coventry factory and adding a number of newly commissioned tools as well. In fact, the company offered a somewhat abbreviated version of its pre-war range, which had included a 20hp model and drophead coupé

This beautifully presented 16hp six-light Saloon from 1947 is remarkable, not only for its condition, but also because it is a LHD example that was exported to Chile.
(WikiMedia Commons/order_242)

A 12hp Tourer is seen here with side screens erected and tonneau cover in place.

The four-light Sports Saloon is shown here with beautiful dark green paintwork. The turn indicator lamps on the bumper are a modern addition.

The 12hp Tourer's canvas top was a very neat fit when in position.
(WikiMedia Commons/Steve Glover)

bodies built by Salmons & Sons (who would, after the war, be known as Tickford). Initially, there were seven post-war Rovers, based on four-cylinder, 10hp and 12hp chassis and on six-cylinder 14hp and 16hp chassis; there were six-light saloon and four-light sports saloon bodies, on all except the 10hp(for which only a saloon was available), and all these bodies deliberately had a similar appearance.

Production began slowly with a pair of 10hp saloons in December 1945, but Rover had ambitions to expand the range. Despite government exhortations to all car makers to limit the variety of models available, and so conserve resources, Rover was ready by early 1947 with an additional model on the 12hp chassis. Probably mainly to appease the government, which was also urging manufacturers of all kinds to focus on building for export in order to rebuild the war-torn economy, the 12 Tourer was described as for export only. It was not, of course: several found owners in Britain. Interestingly, Rover had created this model by buying back a 1934 sports tourer to copy, although there were several differences when production began. The tourers were built on their own production line at Clay Lane, away from the main Rover assembly lines, and provided work for skilled men who had until recently been building military aircraft.

Rover probably called these cars P2

The 12hp Tourer carried its spare wheel concealed within the boot. The Saloons and Sports Saloons had its shape visible on the outside of the boot lid. Once again, the indicator lights and red reflectors are modern additions.
(WikiMedia Commons/Steve Glover)

models, and enthusiasts do so today. The name came from technical chief Maurice Wilks' unsuccessful attempts to create what he called Model P – presumably P for Post-war – that had begun in late 1945. That car did not materialise, but the one that followed it logically became model P2. From the start of 1947, a Clayton-Dewandre heater-demister system became standard, and a modified dashboard even allowed the installation of a radio.

However, production never reached pre-war levels, and by May 1947 the Rover factories were working only four days a week on alternate weeks. To keep the company afloat, Maurice Wilks rapidly designed the Land Rover, which soon outsold Rover cars and would continue to do so for many more years. Without it, Rover would almost certainly have gone under by 1950.

Models: 10hp Saloon, 12hp Saloon, 12hp Sports Saloon, 12hp Tourer, 14hp Saloon, 14hp Sports Saloon, 16hp Saloon, 16hp Sports Saloon.

Engines: (10hp) 1389cc (66.5mm x 100mm) OHV four-cylinder, with approx 48bhp. (12hp) 1496cc (69mm x 100mm) OHV four-cylinder, with approx 53bhp. (14hp) 1901cc (63.5mm x 100mm) OHV six-cylinder; power output not quoted. (16hp) 2147cc (67.5mm x 100mm) OHV six-cylinder, with approx 66bhp.

Gearbox: Four-speed manual with synchromesh on third and fourth, plus freewheel.

Steering, suspension and brakes: Worm-and-nut steering Front beam axle with semi-elliptic leaf springs and hydraulic piston-type dampers Semi-elliptic rear leaf springs on 'live' axle, with hydraulic piston-type dampers Drum brakes all round with mechanical actuation

Main dimensions: Length: 152in. Width: 62in. Height: 62.5in. (Saloon and Sports Saloon) Wheelbase: 105.5in. Track: 50in (front), 51.5in (rear).

Performance and fuel consumption: 14hp: 72mph, approximately 23mpg. 16hp: 77mph, approximately 19mpg.

Production totals: 10hp: 2640 12hp: 4840 (including 200 Tourers). 14hp: 1705 16hp: 4150.

P3 60 and 75 (1948-1949)

Rover's second post-1945 range of cars looked a lot like its predecessors, although that was certainly not for want of trying. Maurice Wilks had tried all kinds of styles for the Model P he had been working on since late 1945, most of them based on the existing Rover bodyshell. Unfortunately, most of them looked exactly like what they were, which was rather desperate attempts to modernise a pre-war design.

During 1947, Wilks realised things had gone on for too long. So he decided to postpone the introduction of an all-new Rover until he could come up with a satisfactory shape for it. In the mean time, the latest Rover engines could be used in a more subtly updated version of the

existing Rover body shape. By this stage, Model P had been followed by P2 (the revived pre-war car), and so the new one logically became P3.

There were to be two different versions of the body, one with four windows (called a Sports Saloon) and one with six windows (called a Saloon). Each of these would be available with two different engines, a 1.6-litre four-cylinder and a 2.1-litre six-cylinder, both of them based on the new IOE (Inlet-Over-Exhaust) design drawn up at the end of the 1930s by Rover's engine designer, Jack Swaine. Wilks also had ambitious plans to put a P3 drophead coupé into production, but although two were built by coachbuilder Salmons-Tickford, and one was displayed at the 1948 Motor Show, no more followed.

Despite a close visual resemblance to the existing P2 models, the new P3 was not as conservative as it looked. Chassis designer Gordon Bashford had drawn up a three-quarters chassis frame that was bolted to the rear of the body just ahead of the rear springs, so removing restrictions on rear axle movement

The P3 looked much like the P2 it replaced, although there were differences, like a more upright grille and a centre fog light as standard. This is the four-light Sports Saloon.

The 60 and 75 were visually indistinguishable from one another, but the model name was carried in two places. One was on the radiator grille ...

From the rear, the P3 also closely resembled its predecessor. This is again a four-light Sports Saloon, the better looking of the two body options. (WikiMedia Common/Steve Glover)

... and the other was on the spare wheel indentation in the boot lid.

that had hindered ride comfort. That frame was also tremendously strong, thanks to its use of box-section members instead of the more common channel-section type. Additional structural strength came from an all-steel body, manufactured for Rover by Pressed Steel but assembled at Solihull.

While the P3 was under development, the British road tax system changed to a flat rate from one based on a (calculated) RAC horsepower rating. So although the plan to introduce 12hp and 16hp models of the P3 went ahead, they were given new names. Reflecting their approximate power outputs, the 12hp became a Rover 60 and the 16hp became a Rover 75. The new engines delivered welcome extra performance and the modified rear suspension improved road comfort.

There was just one problem. The new 60 and 75 may have suited conservative Rover customers in Britain, but the government was focussing on export of manufactured goods to help rebuild

the war-torn economy. Few British buyers could actually obtain a new Rover P3 because most of those built were earmarked to go abroad. Therein lay Rover's problem, because the cars were having to compete for sales with much more modern-looking rivals. So the P3 lasted only for around 18 months in production, and the new P4 could not come soon enough.

There was one more good thing to come out of this period. The four-cylinder engine from the 60 was exactly what Rover needed to power the new Land-Rover (the name was hyphenated in those days), and with modifications it would continue to do so for several years. As for the Land-Rover, it sold so well both at home and abroad that Rover stopped worrying about export sales of their cars and instead began to worry if they could ever make enough Land-Rovers to meet demand.

Models: 60 Saloon, 60 Sports Saloon, 75 Saloon, 75 Sports Saloon.
Engines: (60) 1595cc (69.5mm x 105mm) IOE four-cylinder, with 60bhp.
(75) 2103cc (65.2mm x 105mm) IOE six-cylinder, with 75bhp.
Gearbox: Four-speed manual with synchromesh on third and fourth, plus freewheel.
Steering, suspension and brakes: Recirculating ball steering Independent front suspension with coil springs, anti-roll bar and piston-type dampers. Semi-elliptic rear leaf springs on 'live' axle, with hydraulic telescopic dampers. Drum brakes all round with hydraulic front system and mechanical rear system.
Main dimensions: Length: 171.25in. Width: 63in Height: 62in (Sports Saloon); 65in (Six-light saloon). Wheelbase: 110.5in Track: 51.187in (front), 54.875in (rear).
Performance and fuel consumption: 60: 72mph, approximately 30mpg 75: 75mph, 23-28mpg.
Production totals: 60: 1274. 75: 7835, plus 2 drophead coupés.

The six-light Saloon was deliberately more upright and dignified in appearance. Here is one pictured when new in the showrooms of Annand & Thompson, in Australia.

A single P3 75 was specially bodied by the Swiss coachbuilder Graber as a cabriolet.

P4 60, 75, 80, 90, 95, 100, 105, 105R, 105S and 110 (1949-1964)

Maurice Wilks finally found the visual inspiration he wanted for the all-new post war Rover in the 1947 Studebakers, designed by Raymond Loewy.

These cars were hugely influential all around the world, balancing the projecting bonnet with a projecting boot to give what is often called a 'three-box' design. Wilks also followed American inspiration in using a bench front seat and column gearchange for the new range of cars that became the P4 in Rover nomenclature.

The P4 was introduced in autumn 1949 as a 1950 model, but there was only one version. This was the 75, which had a further-developed version of the six-cylinder engine from the P3 75. With a full-length chassis, these cars were heavier than the P3s they replaced and not as quick, despite several light-alloy panels. They also had a distinctive 'Cyclops eye' fog lamp in the centre of a slatted grille, which was the main cause of overheating problems.

There were some interesting variants in this early period. In 1950, Rover had Tickford build an open version of the P4 body for its experimental gas turbine-powered car, JET 1, which, in 1952, reached 152mph on the Jabbeke highway in Belgium. This probably inspired the two drophead prototypes and a visually related two-door coupé that Tickford built in 1951, but no production followed. And during 1950-1951, the Marauder Car Company (initially called Wilks, Mackie & Co) turned 15 examples of the 75 chassis into Marauders. All these were shortened and some were given tuned engines as well; 14 were bodied as two-seat tourers and one as a two-seat coupé, but the Marauder venture folded when Purchase Tax increased and made the cars unsaleable.

To counter the overheating problem, the 1952 models had a new grille with vertical slats and no foglamp. These cars also had a bigger rear window. Two years later, as post-war restrictions were easing, Rover added new models to the range – a four-cylinder 60 and a more powerful six-cylinder 90. Both these and the 1954 75 gained synchromesh on second gear. They also had a handbrake alongside the driver's seat, but this was not liked and was discontinued after just a year. All these early models had a freewheel in the driveline.

The difficulty that Maurice Wilks had in arriving at the P4 shape, plus the additional burdens on him as engineering chief now that the Land Rover had become a major success, probably persuaded him to seek outside styling help. In late 1952, he commissioned drophead and fixed-head coupé designs from the Italian stylist Pinin Farina on the P4 chassis. The drophead was then copied in Britain to create a production prototype on a 90 chassis, but Rover had too many other commitments to take these designs further.

Meanwhile, Wilks had engaged David Bache to take over styling duties at Rover, and it was Bache who skilfully redrew the P4's boot with a higher crown line to give more space, while adding a three-piece wraparound rear window.

The boot lid on early cars sloped downwards, as on this 1951 Cyclops. The rear window was slightly enlarged a year later, but remained generally similar to the type shown.

The first P4 75s had a central fog light that earned them the nickname of Cyclops. This is a 1951 model.

The 1952 models had a new grille to deal with an overheating problem. This 75 still had a column gearchange.

With this for 1955 came a redesigned engine for the 75, more closely related to the 90's, and for 1956 the 90 had an overdrive option. The 60, 75 and 90 remained visually unchanged until the 1957 season brought modified front wings that incorporated the sidelamps to give a greater resemblance to the forthcoming P5 model. At the same time, a twin-carburettor version of the 90 engine delivered the 105R and 105S, the former with Rover's own Roverdrive automatic gearbox – which did nothing for performance or fuel economy.

The final major visual change came for the 1959 models, bringing both a recessed radiator grille (again inspired by the P5), and new bumpers with bigger over-riders. By this stage, the models available were the 60, 75, 90 and 105, all with manual gearboxes and overdrive (an option on the 60). For 1960, the 100 became the sole six-cylinder car, with the 80 as the four-cylinder

Above: There was never a production convertible, but Rover did commission Italian coachbuilder Pinin Farina to build a prototype in 1952. Finished in gold with a red hood, the car looked stunning. Rover then had a 'production prototype' built on a 90 chassis by Mulliner of Birmingham, but the project was abandoned.

The bigger-engined 90 brought more power from 1953, and had an offset fog lamp as standard. This Wiltshire police car is actually a 75, but has a 90-style fog lamp. (PVEC)

Changed lighting regulations saw the sidelights move to the wing tops for 1954.

For 1955, the rear end was restyled by David Bache, with a three-piece rear window and larger boot. This LHD 90 was exported to the USA.

17

option, using a version of the 2.25-litre OHV engine designed for the 1959-model Series II Land Rover. The 100's engine, meanwhile, was a short-stroke version of the redesigned six-cylinder used in the P5 3-litre. Both cars had disc front brakes.

For the last two years of the P4's life there were only six-cylinder P4s, partly to protect sales of the new four-cylinder P6 saloon introduced in autumn 1963. The models were the 95 (without overdrive) and the 110 (with overdrive and a more powerful engine with Weslake-developed cylinder head). From March 1963, both took on steel-panelled doors in place of the alloy-panelled doors used ever since 1949.

The P4 range was something of an anachronism by the start of the 1960s, not only in looks but its reliance on a separate chassis when most cars had switched to monocoque construction. But it was always much loved by its

The 'suicide' rear doors of the P4 remained long after such designs were considered outmoded. Pictured is a 1959 105 model.
(Simon Brown)

For 1958, the two-tone schemes changed to the style seen here. This is an unusual colour combination, on a 1958 75.

Early two-tone colour schemes had a second colour for the roof, seen here on a 1957 105R.

The final P4 range included the 110, with distinctive wheel trims from the P5 3-litre. This 1964 car was exported to New Zealand when new, and shows the later style of over-riders, used from mid-1959.

largely conservative and older buyers, who valued its solid construction and discreet comfort in the finest Rover tradition.

The P4 range went through several visual changes during its 15-year lifetime, not always associated with changes in model names. To understand these, it is simplest to divide the range into five visual types, as follows (dates refer to model-year, or season):

First type (1950-1951) 'Cyclops eye' foglamp 75.
Second type (1952-1954) Square headlamp fairings, low boot line, sidelamps on wing tops (1954 only) 75 (1952-1954) 60 & 90 (1954).
Third type (1955-1956) Square headlamp fairings, sidelamps on wing tops, raised boot line 60, 75 & 90.
Fourth type (1957-1958) Raised front wing line, flush radiator grille 60, 75, 90, 105R & 105S.
Fifth type (1959-1964) Recessed radiator grille, big over-riders 60, 75, 90 & 105 (1959) 80 & 100 (1960-1962) 95 & 110 (1963-1964).
Models: 60, 75, 80, 90, 95, 100, 105, 105R, 105S, 110 (all Saloons).
Engines: (60) 1997cc (77.8 x 105mm) IOE four-cylinder, with 60bhp. (75) 2103cc (65.2mm x 105mm) IOE six-cylinder, with 75bhp. (1950-1954) 2230cc (73.025mm x 88.9mm) IOE six-cylinder, with 80bhp. (1955-1959) (80) 2286cc (90.47mm x 88.8mm) OHV four-cylinder, with 77bhp. (90) 2638cc (73.025mm x 105mm) IOE six-cylinder, with 90bhp. (1954-1955) or 93bhp (1956-1959) (95) 2625cc (77.8mm x 92.075mm) IOE six-cylinder, with 102bhp. (100) 2625cc (77.8mm x 92.075mm) IOE six-cylinder, with 104bhp. (105, 105R & 105S) 2638cc (73.025mm x 105mm) IOE six-cylinder, with 108bhp. (110) 2625cc (77.8mm x 92.075mm) IOE six-cylinder, with 123bhp.
Gearbox: Four-speed manual with synchromesh on third and fourth (1950-1953), or second, third and fourth (1954-1964); freewheel (1949-1959) or overdrive (optional from 1956, standard on 75 and 90 from 1957) Roverdrive two-speed automatic with automatic overdrive on 105R.
Steering, suspension and brakes: Recirculating ball steering Independent front suspension with coil springs, anti-roll bar and hydraulic telescopic dampers. Semi-elliptic rear leaf springs on 'live' axle, with hydraulic telescopic dampers. Drum brakes all round with hydraulic system (1950-1959); disc brakes on front wheels (1960-1964); servo assistance on 90 with overdrive and on all 80, 95, 100, 105, 105R, 105S and 110.
Main dimensions: Length: 178.25in (1950-1958); 178.625in (1959-1964). Width: 65.625in. Height: 63.75in. Wheelbase: 111in. Track: 52in (front), 51.5in (rear).
Performance and fuel consumption: 60: 77mph, 29mpg 75: 82mph, 23mpg (2103cc) 85mph, 24mpg (2230cc) 80: 85mph, 22mpg 90: 84mph, 22mpg 95: 94mph, 22mpg 100: 92mph, 22mpg 105R: 94mph, 23mpg 105/105S: 95mph, 22mpg 110: 100mph, 24mpg.
Production totals: 60: 9666 75: 43,241 (including 3 dropheads and 1 coupé) 80: 5900 90: 35,903 (including 1 drophead) 95: 3680 100: 16,521 105: 2026 105R: 3540 105S: 5215 110: 4620.

The Marauder sports car was based on a cut-down P4 75 chassis. This is the fifth example built.

P5 3-LITRE (1958-1967) AND P5B 3.5-LITRE (1967-1973)

By the early 1950s, the profits from booming Land Rover sales were encouraging the Rover Company to consider expansion, and the initial plan was to build a car that was smaller and cheaper than P4, but would sell alongside it in larger volumes. However, continuing demand for Land Rovers made it increasingly clear that there was not enough room on the Solihull factory site to build a larger-volume saloon range. So the idea of P5 as a 'small' car was abandoned, and P5 was instead re-imagined as a more expensive car than P4, selling alongside it in smaller volumes.

By the mid-1950s, P5 was being designed as a luxury-class saloon. Styling was by David Bache, while Gordon Bashford proposed Rover's first all-steel monocoque construction for the body, with a substantial sub-frame to support the engine, gearbox and front suspension. The existing six-cylinder IOE engine was re-engineered with seven main bearings and a 3-litre capacity, and the result was announced as the Rover 3-litre in autumn 1958. Both manual and automatic gearboxes were available, the latter a conventional Borg Warner three-speed, and the former typically accompanied by overdrive.

Disc front brakes were added for 1961, but it was already clear that the 3-litre needed power-assisted steering, while its modern but rather fussy interior trim was expensive and tricky to manufacture. So when the Mk IA model arrived for the 1962 model-year (making the first cars into Mk I types), it had a number of revisions, with a more conventional interior and a lower ride height as well as PAS as standard.

There were some interesting experiments

Two-tone combinations were popular on 3-litres right through to the mid-1960s. This very early Mk I shows the P4-style hubcaps used on those models – and a Rover badge on the front wings that was deleted from production cars.

This is the Mk IA/ Mk II style of grille badging. Of course, it normally read "Rover 3 Litre," but this is one of the very rare smaller-engined cars built for Austria.

Only the Mk I cars had this style of Rover name on the grille, although the plastic Viking ship badge would be used up to 1965.

The Mk II 3-litre was introduced in spring 1962, and was a very well-resolved improvement on the original design. This is actually a late Mk IIC type, with a door mirror that was not standard. Note the full-size wheel trims, introduced with the Mk IA models.

in these early years. Rover evaluated a 3-litre estate in 1959, and there were three drophead conversions, by Chapron (1962), Graber (1963) and FLM Panelcraft (1965). All of these remained unique. From 1962, there were P5 saloons for export with the 2.6-litre P4 engine, and also with a special short-stroke 2.4-litre engine, but both were short-lived.

The next step for mainstream production was to a Mk II in April 1962, which answered

Also new in spring 1962 was the Coupé model, with raked front and rear screens and a lower roofline. This publicity picture actually shows a prototype.

This rear view of a Mk III Saloon shows the three 'pips' (see inset) at the end of the side trim that designated Mk III models.

Right: No convertible P5s were built at the factory, but a few aftermarket conversions were done. The most attractive was the first, by the French coachbuilder Henri Chapron in 1962.

The larger Viking ship badge from the P6 was incorporated in the grille for the Mk III models, and the side trim strips were changed. This is a 1966 Coupé.

criticisms of the earlier cars with more power and performance from a new cylinder head developed with assistance from tuning specialist Harry Weslake. The Mk II saloons were accompanied by a new four-door Coupé model, with a lower roof and more rakish lines, although it brought no extra power. Saloon and Coupé then went through minor revisions over the next few years: the first Mk IIs were, strictly, Mk IIA types, and were followed by Mk IIB models in 1963 and then by Mk IIC models in 1964. The main improvement for the Mk IIC was a revised engine with larger main bearings.

To keep the P5 as modern as possible, the Mk III from autumn 1965 had revised side trims and a larger grille badge, plus redesigned seats which followed the shape of those in Rover's new 2000 saloons. But the Mk III was really a holding operation, because a new model that would provide all the performance customers wanted was already in preparation.

The new model arrived in autumn 1967 with the name 'Rover 3.5-litre,' which reflected the capacity of its new engine. This was Rover's new

This Mk II was converted to drophead from for a private customer by London coachbuilder FLM Panelcraft in 1965.

Two-tone paint was available on Coupé models of the P5B right to the end of production.

The V8-engined P5B models were characterised by twin foglights built into the front wings, another new grille badge, chromed Rostyle wheels and another variation of the side trim. Several went to the Government car fleet, and others, like this one, became military staff cars.

all-aluminium V8, which the company had bought from General Motors' Buick division in America, developing it to suit British manufacturing methods and the requirements of Rover cars. The new models were called P5B types, the B standing for Buick. Saloon and Coupé were distinguished by a new front with fog lamps recessed into the front wings and a new, gold-coloured grille badge. There were chromed Rostyle wheels with an almost sporty design, minor changes to the side trims, and a new centre console for the selector of the standard automatic gearbox.

Rover expected to replace the 3.5-litre (renamed a 3½-litre in 1969, although with no badge changes) in 1971 with the new P8 saloon then under development, but its masters at British Leyland cancelled the new car at the last minute, fearing a clash with existing Jaguar saloons. So the P5B remained in production until 1973, a glorious anachronism in its final years but still highly respected as a grand or formal saloon. Many belonged to the government car fleet or were used to transport high-ranking military officers, and even HM The Queen drove one, which she claimed was her favourite car.

Models: 3-litre Saloon, 3-litre Coupé; 3.5-litre Saloon, 3.5-litre Coupé; 2.4-litre Saloon (export only); 2.6-litre Saloon (export only).
Engines: (3-litre) 2995cc (77.8 x 105mm) IOE six-cylinder, with 115bhp (1959-1963), 134bhp (1963-1967, manual) or 129bhp (1963-1967, automatic) (3.5-litre) 3528cc (88.9 x 71.1mm) OHV V8, with 184bhp. (Brake horsepower figures are quoted to SAE standards, as was the practice of the time. Those for the V8 engine are therefore higher than the figures for the P6B and later V8s, which are quoted to stricter DIN standards.)
Gearbox: Four-speed manual with optional overdrive (3-litre only). Three-speed automatic.
Steering, suspension and brakes: Recirculating ball steering; power assistance optional (1961), then standard on Coupé from 1962 and on Saloon from 1965. Front suspension with torsion bars, anti-roll bar and hydraulic telescopic dampers. Semi-elliptic rear leaf springs on 'live' axle, with hydraulic telescopic dampers. Drum brakes all round (1958-1960); disc brakes on front wheels (1960-1973); servo assistance standard.

Main dimensions: Length: 186.5in. Width: 70in. Height: 60.25in (1958-1962) 59.25in. (Saloon from 1962) 56.75in (Coupé). Wheelbase: 110.5in Track:55in (front), 56in (rear).
Performance and fuel consumption: 3-litre: 93-96mph, 16-24mpg. (Mk I and Mk IA) 102-108mph, 15-22mpg. (Mk II and Mk III) 3.5-litre: 110mph, 20-23mpg.
Production totals: 3-litre: 48,385 (Saloon 40,402; Coupé 7983). 2.4-litre: 25. 2.6-litre: 131. 3.5-litre: 20,600 (Saloon 11,501; Coupé 9099).

P6 and P6B (1963-1977)

The P6 story can be traced right back to 1953, when Rover started to look at building a second range of saloon cars, smaller and cheaper than the existing P4 models. That plan was abandoned when it became clear that there was no room at Solihull to build a high-volume car model, and the 'second range' was re-envisaged as a low-volume, more expensive car, which became the P5.

By the mid-1950s, Rover was starting to think about a model to replace the P4, and planning focussed on an ultra-modern lightweight saloon that would be smaller than P4 but no less luxurious. While Maurice Wilks led the engineering and design, there was input from some of Rover's younger engineers as well, notably Peter Wilks and Spen King.

Gordon Bashford drew up the new structure as a base unit to which unstressed outer panels could be added, drawing inspiration from the

The original 2000 had very clean lines that depended on shape rather than adornment. This is a 1964 model.

Citroën DS. David Bache was responsible for the clean, sculpted styling, and Jack Swaine drew up a new four-cylinder engine. Rear suspension had a De Dion layout, while the unusual front suspension was designed around a wide gas turbine engine, which was prototyped but did not enter production. Brakes were discs all round.

The new car was introduced in autumn 1963 and was called the Rover 2000. It created something of a sensation at the time and was widely praised – even though, in truth, both rear-seat legroom and boot space were minimal. It caught the wave of a change in the market, which was now calling for smart 'executive' saloons

Not much changed for the 2000TC, of which this is a 1966 example. Note the TC badges on the wing and bonnet.

rather than old-style large cars like the P4, and became a big success.

Rover recognised that the P6's excellent handling could cope with more power, and were already investigating options when the car was launched. One option was a six-cylinder engine (and the outcome of that is explained in the next section); another was a twin-carburettor version of the 2-litre four-cylinder. The 2000TC was announced alongside the basic 2000 in 1966, and its extra performance won the P6 more friends. So did the 2000 Automatic, released a few months later, although performance was definitely not its strong suit. From autumn 1967, the single-carburettor cars were re-named 2000SC and 2000SC Automatic.

Meanwhile, Rover had bought the manufacturing and development rights to the 3.5-litre all-alloy V8 designed by General Motors. That engine fitted into the P6 programme as the new top option, and the new P6B (B for Buick), or 3500 model, was introduced in April 1968. Even though it came only with an automatic gearbox because Rover had not developed a satisfactory manual alternative, it was, once again, a big sales success. The only blot on the horizon was slow sales in the USA, where a special 3500S model

This early 3500 shows the characteristics of the model: rubber-faced over-riders, fatter tyres, a bonnet 'eyebrow', and distinguishing badges. The wheel trims with twin centre rings were adopted for all P6 and P6B models in 1968.

suffered from an undersized dealer network – which had also hindered sales of the four-cylinder cars. So North American sales of the P6 and P6B models were discontinued in 1971.

Face-lifted models arrived in 1970, distinguished mainly by a new black plastic grille, a bonnet with twin 'power bulges', bright side trims, and black vinyl quarter-panel coverings. Then in 1971 came a manual-gearbox V8 model, called the 3500S. This was distinguished by a full vinyl roof covering and by special wheel trims, while its superb performance gave a new dimension to the public image of Rover. It became a favourite as a high-speed patrol car with police forces in Britain.

The final major changes were made in autumn 1973. The 2000s were all replaced by 2200 models with a big-bore version of the same engine, and these were called 2200SC, 2200

The rear end was mostly unchanged, although there were variations of badging and other details. Despite the registration number, this is a 1970-model 2000 Automatic.

The 1971-season face-lift was established by the time of this 1972-model 3500S, which shows the model's special wheel trims

Automatic and 2200TC; the engine's extra torque vastly improved the Automatic model. The 3500 and 3500S were slightly detuned to take lower-quality petrol, and their overall specifications were made more similar to one another. A final special edition called the 3500 VIP was released in late 1975, with either silver paint intended for the SD1 cars that would take over from mid-1976, or the latest Brasilia brown. The last Rover P6 was then assembled at Solihull in March 1977.

Rover evaluated a drophead conversion in 1965, which they commissioned from FLM Panelcraft. It remained unique (although there have been several DIY conversions in more recent years). From 1968, an estate derivative of the P6 and P6B models was available as a Rover-approved conversion. It was designed and built by FLM Panelcraft, although the build of later examples (sold through HR Owen) was sub-contracted to Crayford. Graber built a handful of coupés and convertibles in the mid-1960s, and Zagato built one special coupé in 1966. There was a David Bache-designed hatchback coupé in 1967, intended for Rover's subsidiary Alvis, and Chapron also converted one 3500 into a landaulet in the 1970s.

Models: 2000, 2000SC, 2000 Automatic, 2000SC Automatic, 2000TC, 2200SC, 2200SC Automatic, 2200TC, 3500 3500S (Federal), 3500S.
Engines: 2000: 1978cc (85.7 x 85.7mm) OHC four-cylinder, with 90bhp 2000TC: 1978cc (85.7 x 85.7mm) OHC four-cylinder, with 110bhp 2200: 2204cc (90.5 x 85.7mm) OHC four-cylinder, with 98bhp 2200TC: 2204cc (90.5 x 85.7mm) OHC four-cylinder, with 115bhp 3500 & 3500S: 3528cc (88.9 x 71.1mm) OHC V8, with 144bhp (Brake horse power figures are quoted to DIN standards).
Gearbox: Four-speed all-synchromesh manual Three-speed automatic.
Steering, suspension and brakes: Worm-and-roller steering; power assistance on some V8 models Independent front suspension with transverse lower links, leading upper links and horizontal coil springs; hydraulic telescopic dampers and anti-roll bar Independent rear suspension with De Dion tube, stabiliser rod, Watts linkage and coil springs; hydraulic telescopic dampers Disc brakes all round with standard servo assistance.
Main dimensions: Length: 178.5in; 179.75in with

rubber-faced over-riders. Width: 66in. Height: 54.75in (four-cylinders); 55.75in (V8 models). Wheelbase: 103.375in. Track: 53.375in (front), 52.5in (rear).

Performance and fuel consumption: 2000: 102mph, 25mpg, 0-60mph in 15.1 sec 2000 Auto: 94mph, 22mpg, 0-60mph in 18.0 sec 2000TC: 107mph, 25mpg, 0-60mph in 11.9sec. 2200SC: 101mph, 29mpg, 0-60mph in 13.4 sec. 2200 Auto: 101mph, 22mpg, 0-60mph in 14.5 sec. 2200TC:107mph, 24mpg, 0-60mph in 11.4 sec. 3500: 114mph, 19mpg, 0-60mph in 10.5 sec. 3500S: 122mph, 23mpg, 0-60mph in 9.1 sec. Production totals: 327,208 (official figure).

P6BS and P9 (1966-1969)

As Rover got to grips with its new V8 engine in the mid-1960s, it became very clear that the power available from it opened several new possibilities. One of those was for a

This 2200SC has the wheel trims, black sills and vinyl quarter-pillars introduced on facelift cars, and the door mirror introduced in 1973.

Vinyl roofs were normally black, but a brown option became available and is seen here on a 1974 3500; the sills were painted brown to match.

high-performance sports car and, although there was no officially approved budget for the project, Spen King and his chassis designer Gordon Bashford got together in their spare time to draw up just such a car. With a V8 engine mounted amidships just behind the seats, a fixed roof and many mechanical elements from the production P6 saloons, the single prototype was a highly impressive machine.

King and Bashford had initially called it the BS (Buick Special), but the name was later changed to P6BS. The car was then shown to some motoring magazines just before the P6B 3500 was announced in 1968, to whet their appetites for the forthcoming new model. It was also shipped over to the USA, where it

This rear view shows a late 2200SC, with plate-type badges and the standard black vinyl pillars. The fog guard lamps under the bumper were an extra.

London coachbuilder FLM Panelcraft developed an estate conversion which was granted Rover approval; Crayford later built some to the same design, and London dealer HR Owen marketed them as the Owen conversion. Most, like this one, were built from V8-engined cars; there were about 160 in all.

was shown at the New York International Motor Show under the name of the Leyland GE, those letters standing for Group Experimental. There were already tentative production plans, and reactions to the prototype persuaded

Rover commissioned Panelcraft to build a drophead P6 after seeing the P5 drophead it had built for a private customer. The car was converted from a standard 2000 saloon.

Rover to look harder at these. David Bache designed a most attractive body shape in place of the original rough-and-ready one by King and Bashford, and a formal project was planned, with the car now known as the P9. A full-size styling mock-up was produced, and although this carried Rover badges, there was talk of releasing it with the badges of Rover's Alvis subsidiary. It would have followed the long line of sporting cars that had just ended production there.

However, Jaguar's Sir William Lyons persuaded the British Leyland Board that the P9 represented an unacceptable threat to sales of his E-type, while Triumph's George Turnbull was concerned that it might eat into sales for the Stag grand tourer. So, in 1969, Rover was instructed to stop work on it. The P6BS prototype and a 1/8 scale styling model for the P9 have both survived, and belong to the British Motor Museum at Gaydon.

Swiss coachbuilder Graber did a number of coupé and cabriolet conversions between 1966 and 1968. This coupé was based on a 3500.

Rover's David Bache asked Zagato to build this one-off fastback coupé from a twin-carburettor 2000 in 1966. It was known as the Rover TCZ.

Bache was also working on a hatchback coupé himself. The single prototype was constructed by the Harold Radford coachworks in London from a twin-carburettor 2000, although production cars would probably have had V8 engines. The car was intended to become a new model for Alvis, and the prototype has always been affectionately known as Gladys. (WikiMedia Commons/Buch-t)

In 1968, the sole prototype of the P6BS was shipped out to the USA, where this picture was taken. At this stage, the car was wearing Minilite alloy wheels.

This rear view was also taken during the car's trip to the USA. The V8 engine was offset to one side, and the carburettors were crudely concealed under a perspex cover.

The 1/8 scale model of David Bache's proposed P9 survives in the Heritage Collection at the British Motor Museum.

P7 (1962-1969)

As originally conceived, the P7 was a high-performance development of the P6 saloon, but its development was aborted when Rover bought the 3.5-litre V8 engine from General Motors. This engine gave them a more cost-effective way of achieving the same end than the one they had been working on.

A six-cylinder version of P6 was under consideration as early as 1957, but priority was given to the four-cylinder car, and the idea of a six-cylinder alternative seems to have been forgotten. The reason for its revival may well have been Rover's discovery that Triumph were planning a six-cylinder engine for their new saloon that was aimed at the same group of buyers as the Rover P6.

The only surviving P7 is P7/4, which was the last of the OHC six-cylinder prototypes in the original project. The car had an interim front end design with lengthened front wings and bonnet. (RSR)

By then, the P6 base unit had been designed around the four-cylinder engine, and its engine bay was too short to take a six-cylinder. Nevertheless, at the end of 1960 the Rover Board approved development of a six-cylinder P6 – which would be different enough from the parent car to merit the new development code of P7. Serious work began in 1962 as development of the four-cylinder car was ending, and by early 1963 P7 was envisaged as a long-nose version of the P6. The six-cylinder engine was designed as essentially one-and-a-half four-cylinder OHC types, with a swept volume of around 3.0 litres, and the design target was for the single-carburettor version to give a 128mph maximum speed. Test examples, some with multiple carburettors, exceeded that by quite some margin.

After four prototypes had been built, the cost of tooling up for the new front end began to look prohibitive. Rover tried alternatives: during 1964, one experimental car ran with an IOE six-cylinder engine in a standard-length engine bay. At about the same time, a 2.5-litre five-cylinder version of the OHC engine was also tried, the thinking being that this was shorter than the six-cylinder. However, all work on the five-cylinder and six-cylinder P7s was suspended when it became clear that the new V8 engine would not only deliver the desired performance but would also need minimal front-end modifications.

This was the six-cylinder engine, which was, in effect, one and a half of the Rover 2000 four-cylinder types...

... and this was the experimental five-cylinder, again based on the Rover 2000's OHC type. The block, cylinder head and top cover were all made by cutting and shutting two four-cylinder types – hence the very visible weld lines.

Development of the V8-engined P6 was carried forward under the P6B name, but the P7 name was now applied to a series of experimental cars built to test elements of the planned P8 and, later, P10 models. Most were based on P6s, but one was based on a P5 3-litre; several had the twin-wishbone front suspension tried on an earlier P7 and now intended for P8. The last of them (known as P7F) was probably built in 1969, and had a 'live' rear axle to simulate the P10 design. Just one P7 has survived. It is number P7/4, the last of the long-nose cars designed around the new six-cylinder engine.

P8 (1964-1971)

During 1965, the Rover Board approved a new-model strategy that Spen King had outlined the previous year. Reasoning that Rover could not afford to develop separate designs to replace its existing P5 and P6 saloons, he proposed a single design that could be adapted to do both jobs. Engine sizes and equipment levels would distinguish top models from less expensive ones.

So work began on P8, which was to have a larger passenger cabin than P6 but the same overall size as that car. Work was proceeding along these lines when Rover merged with the Leyland Motor Corporation in 1966. Leyland reviewed its product plans, and decided that it wanted Rover to produce a luxury flagship model to rival Jaguar (which was not then part of the Leyland group). So P8 was scaled up to become a larger and technically more ambitious design,

while another new model – later called P10 – was planned as the eventual P6 replacement. All this became much more complicated when Leyland merged with British Motor Holdings and Jaguar in 1968. Nevertheless, the potential in-house clash between P8 and Jaguar was ignored, and P8 development went ahead. Key features were a P6-like base unit construction, a 4.4-litre version of the V8 engine in addition to the 3.5-litre size, and a Citroën-style high-pressure hydraulic system for the brakes. A Station Wagon variant was under consideration for the future, and the first P8 prototype was completed in summer 1970. Six more would be built, in 1970 and 1971.

Everything was on course for a launch date of autumn 1971, but a few months before that, British Leyland reviewed expenditure and the forward plans of all its constituent companies. It became clear that the Rover P8 would be a direct competitor for Jaguar's XJ6, and after Jaguar's Sir William Lyons argued his corner forcefully (as he had a few months earlier over the potential clash between the Jaguar E-type and the Rover P9), the P8 project was cancelled. The axe fell in March 1971, as the seventh prototype was still being built.

That seventh prototype is now the only surviving P8, and belongs to the British Motor Museum at Gaydon. However, the car was badly damaged while being transported in the mid-1990s and was not on display at the time of writing.

The sole surviving P8 prototype was damaged in the early days of its preservation, but at the time of writing was due to be refurbished. Although the car looks battered in this photograph, its essential lines are clear. (Nick Dunning)

The car's condition does not do its shape justice, but this rear view of the surviving prototype shows how a large impact-absorbing plastic moulding was to be used at the rear. There would have been a 'nose' of similar material as well. (Nick Dunning)

SD1 (1976-1986)

Rover started work on a replacement for the P6 range in 1969, giving it the code-name of P10. However, by 1971 British Leyland had become concerned about a clash between this car and the planned new Triumph saloon, which was being developed as the Puma. The BL Board reviewed both projects and selected the Rover to go ahead, while Triumph was given the job of designing new engines for what was briefly known as RT1 (Rover-Triumph no1). That autumn, it was renamed SD1, in anticipation of the new Specialist Division that would be formally created in 1972, with an amalgamated Rover-Triumph central to it.

Rover's David Bache had some advanced ideas for the SD1, and settled on making it a hatchback, which was rare among executive-class cars. His early designs were disappointing, but by borrowing ideas from Italian supercars of the time, he created a smooth, distinctive and timeless shape for the new Rover, which was introduced in summer 1976. All the early cars were 3500 models with the V8 engine; six-cylinder 2300 and 2600 models with the new Triumph engine followed in spring 1977. Despite the excellence of the design, poor build quality and the spartan interior (with neither leather nor wood) deterred many customers. By summer 1979, Rover had realised that buyers still expected all the traditional Rover qualities, and introduced a more luxurious V8-S model, adding a traditional Rover grille badge as well.

A year later came a top-model 3500 Vanden Plas, with leather but still no wood, while alternative (and improved) equipment levels

delivered a wider range of models: 2300, 2300S, 2600, 2600S, and 3500SE. Meanwhile, the SD1 had also been launched in the USA, where the familiar problems of a sparse dealer network and British Leyland standards of quality let it down badly. It was withdrawn from that market after a year.

There were major changes for the 1982 models, which were face-lifted with flush-fitting headlights, apron spoilers on most models, and a deeper tailgate window. Also new were an entry-level 2000 model and a diesel 2400SD Turbo, with an engine bought in from Italian manufacturer VM; this arrived in spring 1982 for continental Europe and October for the UK. More importantly, production was transferred from Solihull to the newly refurbished Morris works at Cowley, which delivered vastly improved quality. A motorsport programme had been established during 1980 and was improving the SD1's image, and from autumn 1982 there was a

The early cars had a straight lower edge to the tailgate window. This is a 1978 3500.

The original interior was almost minimalist, and lacked the wood and leather that Rover buyers expected.

The SD1 was an extraordinarily good-looking car, as this early 3500 shows. The 'skeletal' Viking ship badge on the nose proved controversial.

'homologation special' Rover Vitesse model, with an injected version of the V8 engine.

The range was strengthened in autumn 1983 by the addition of a 2600SE, and although there were trim changes a year later, the major novelties were held over until May 1984. The 2600SE and 3500SE models were discontinued, and a new 2600 Vanden Plas arrived. So did a 3500 Vanden Plas EFi, combining the Vitesse engine with the top luxury specification; it was inspired by customer demand (met during 1983) for an automatic version of the Vitesse. Equipment upgrades in October 1984 helped maintain sales, and from autumn 1985 the Vitesse took on a new front spoiler and a 'twin plenum' (actually twin-throttle) engine that was

needed to homologate a similar change to the race cars. Production was gradually wound down during the 1986 model-year, although a few examples remained in the showrooms into 1987, after the introduction of their Rover 800 successors.

Models: 2000, 2300, 2300S, 2400SD Turbo, 2600, 2600S, 2600SE, 2600 Vanden Plas, 3500, V8-S, 3500SE, 3500 Vanden Plas, Vitesse, Vanden Plas EFi.

Engines: 2000: 1994cc (84.45 x 71.1mm) O-series SOHC four-cylinder, with 101bhp. 2300: 2350cc (81 x 76mm) PE146 SOHC six-cylinder, with 123bhp. 2400: 2393cc (92 x 90mm) VM HR492 four-cylinder turbocharged diesel, with 90bhp. 2600:

From summer 1979, a more traditional Viking ship badge was fitted on the nose. This is a V8-S model, with gold-finished alloy wheels.

The 1981-model 3500 Vanden Plas had dark-painted alloy wheel centres, a side bump strip and headlamp washers as standard.

The high-performance Vitesse came with cross-spoke alloy wheels, a black tail spoiler, and side decals to advertise what it was – although these could be deleted. (Craig Pusey)

2597cc (81 x 84mm) PE166 SOHC six-cylinder, with 136bhp. 3500: 3528cc (88.9 x 71.1mm) SOHC V8, with 155bhp. Vitesse & VdP EFi: 3528cc (88.9 x 71.1mm) SOHC V8, with 190bhp. (Brake horse power figures are quoted to DIN standards. Note that a different, locally-built 2.6-litre engine with 110bhp was used in South Africa.)

Gearbox: Four-speed all-synchromesh manual Five-speed all-synchromesh manual Three-speed automatic.

Steering, suspension and brakes: Rack-and-pinion steering with power assistance on most models. Independent front suspension with MacPherson struts, lower links, anti-roll bar and hydraulic telescopic dampers. Rear axle with torque tube, trailing arms, Watts linkage, coil springs and hydraulic telescopic dampers (self-levelling struts on some models). Front disc brakes and rear drums on most models; ventilated front discs on Vitesse and Vanden Plas EFi; standard servo assistance.

Main dimensions: Length: 4724mm/186in. 4750mm/187in with headlamp washers. Width: 1778mm/70in. Height: 1397mm/55in. Wheelbase: 2814mm/110.8in. Track: 1500mm/59.1in (front and rear) with steel wheels. 1506mm/59.3in (front and rear) with alloy wheels.

Performance and fuel consumption: 2000: 108mph, 23mpg, 0-60mph in 12.4 sec. 2400: 103mph, 29mpg, 0-60mph in 14.2 sec. 2600: 120mph, 23mpg, 0-60mph in 9.0 sec. 3500: 121mph, 20mpg, 0-60mph in 9.6 sec. (automatic) Vitesse: 133mph, 21mpg, 0-60mph in 7.6 sec.

Production total: 303,345

The new bumpers, alloy wheels and front spoiler are seen here on a face-lifted 3500 Vanden Plas from 1982.

The SD1 was a favourite as a police motorway patrol car. This Thames Valley 3500SE shows the deeper rear window of the face-lift cars, with its standard wash-wipe system.
(Thames Valley Police)

More comprehensive instrumentation and better interior materials were welcomed on the face-lifted cars, where wood and leather were both available.

The 1986-model Vitesse – most of which were Twin Plenum cars – had a different front spoiler.
(Rob Hafkamp)

Although estate prototypes of the SD1 were built, no production followed.

Australian Quintet (1983-1985)

The Rover Quintet was the first of two Rover-badged models sold in Australia that were not available anywhere else in the world. Both were derivatives of Honda models with front-wheel drive and transverse engines.

When British Leyland's Australian branch (then called Jaguar Rover Australia) needed a medium-sized hatchback to strengthen its market presence, no model was available to fit the bill. However, in the UK a precedent had been set by the Triumph Acclaim, which was a Honda product that had simply been re-badged. In Australia, Honda was already selling the three-door version of the Honda Quint (called the Quintet in the UK) with its own badges, but the company also had a five-door version in production. So JRA agreed to import Japanese-built five-door models, add Rover badges, and sell them from mid-1983 as the Rover Quintet. Publicity called them the 'economy-size' Rover, and they became the first Rover-badged Hondas.

The Rover Quintet had very few changes from the basic Japanese specification. Apart from its Rover badges, it had only an improved interior with special velour upholstery and a wood-grain dashboard. The Quintet had the same 1.6-litre four-cylinder engine as the Japanese Quint, with the option of five-speed manual or three-speed automatic gearboxes. Production ended in 1985 when the Quint went out of production in Japan. The Rover Quintet was replaced by the Rover 416i, again a re-badged Honda, by which time British Leyland had been re-named the Rover

Group.

Models: Quintet manual, Quintet automatic.
Engine: 1602cc Honda EP (77 x 86mm) SOHC four-cylinder, with 79bhp.
Gearboxes: Five-speed Honda manual. Three-speed Honda semi-automatic.
Steering, suspension and brakes: Rack and pinion steering with standard power assistance. Independent front suspension with MacPherson struts, coil springs, anti-roll bar, and hydraulic telescopic dampers. Independent rear suspension with MacPherson struts, coil springs, anti-roll bar, and hydraulic telescopic dampers. Disc front brakes and drum rear brakes, with servo assistance standard.
Main dimensions: Length: 4105mm/161.6in. Width: 1615mm/63.6in Height: 1355mm/53.3in. Wheelbase: 2360mm/92.9in. Track: 1360mm/53.5in (front), 1380mm/54.3in (rear).
Performance and fuel consumption: Manual: 105mph, 9.1 litres/100km (31mpg), 0-100km/h (62mph) in 15.3sec.
Production total: No figures available.

JRA made play of the fact that the car was a hatchback in their advertising – just like its big brother, the SD1.

The Rover Quintet was a fairly typical Japanese hatchback of the early 1980s in appearance.

The dashboard was typically Honda, although wood trim went some way to supporting the Rover identity.

200, first series (1984-1989)

The Triumph Acclaim, a badge-engineered Honda Ballade that had been introduced in 1981, had been a huge success for Austin Rover, not least because of excellent reliability. So it was logical to replace it with another Honda-derived car when the Japanese company had its new model ready. The deal involved Austin Rover building bodyshells for European versions of the new Honda Ballade at its Longbridge factory, alongside its own versions of the car.

Within Austin Rover, the car was still being called the "Acclaim face-lift" as late as March 1984, and although some engineers also called it SD3, that name never seems to have been official. (SD1 was of course the big Rover hatchback, while SD2 was the aborted replacement for the Triumph Dolomite range.) In the meantime, the Triumph name was on the way out – the decision to drop it had been taken

The lines of the first 200 series were sharp and chiselled, and something of a shock to long-term Rover buyers. This is an early 213 base model, with styled steel wheels.

This is an early 216S, its wheel trims being a recognition feature.

by mid-1982 – and Austin Rover management decided that the new small saloon should fit more comfortably within the company name and become a Rover.

Associated with this was a plan to exploit its passenger cabin's extra size over the Acclaim by designing a unique interior with an up-market appeal worthy of the Rover name. So when the new car was introduced in June 1984, it delivered a double dose of culture shock. Not only was this the first front-wheel-drive Rover (with the exception of the Australia-only Quintet), but it was also the first Rover in public memory that was not a large car. On top of that came a new style of model designation. Inspired by the BMW example, Austin Rover called it a 200 series, the engine size being added BMW-style to give designations of 213 and 216.

The first cars were all 213 models with Honda engines and Honda manual gearboxes; they came as 213, 213S and 213SE. But Austin Rover also planned versions with its own S-series engine, which arrived in May 1985. Standard models were the 216S and 216SE. There were also 216 Vanden Plas and 216 Vitesse models, with a more powerful fuel-injected version of the S-series engine; the Vanden Plas model had a wood and leather interior, while the Vitesse had a deliberately sporty look. As the 1.6-litre models arrived, so the 213SE became automatic-only, and its three-speed Honda gearbox became an option for the 213S; the 216 Vanden Plas, meanwhile, could have a four-speed automatic.

Although the all-alloy Honda engine was much more refined than the S-series, the British engine added welcome performance. The Honda suspension design gave a disappointing ride and only average handling, despite British attempts to improve it; but in due course, Honda adopted the Austin Rover changes for its own Ballade models as well. Meanwhile, both 200 models found a ready market, and although the car was sized mid-way between the Maestro and Montego, it sold at a higher price than either. More importantly, it was perceived as an expensive car, amply justifying the Rover branding, while reliability was generally exemplary.

A face-lift followed in 1987, bringing a deeper boot lid opening, extra equipment and an improved dashboard, and – against all expectations – sales actually increased, so that 1988 became the best-ever year for 200-series production and 1989 the best-ever year for UK sales. Production at Longbridge ended in mid-1989, giving way to the R8 second-generation 200 range.

Models: 213, 213S, 213SE; 216S, 216SE, 216 Vanden Plas EFi, 216 Vitesse.
Engines: 213: 1342cc Honda EV2 (74 x 78mm) SOHC 12-valve four-cylinder, with 71PS. 216S &SE: 1598cc Austin Rover S-series (76.2 x 87.6mm) SOHC four-cylinder, with 86PS. 216 VdP & Vitesse: 1588cc Austin Rover S-series (76.2 x 87.6mm) SOHC four-cylinder, with 103PS.
Gearboxes: Five-speed Honda manual Three-speed automatic optional (213 SE only). Four-speed automatic optional (216 Vanden Plas only).
Steering, suspension and brakes: Rack and pinion steering. Front suspension with struts, torsion bar springs and telescopic dampers. Semi-independent rear suspension with trailing arms, axle tube and swivelling hub bearings; Panhard rod and co-axial coil springs with gas dampers. Disc front brakes and drum rear brakes with standard power assistance.
Main dimensions: Length: 4156mm/163.6in. Width: 1623mm/63.9in. Height: 1378mm/54.3in. Wheelbase: 2450mm/96.5in. Track: 1400mm/55.1in (front), 1415mm/55.7in (rear).
Performance and fuel consumption: 213: 96mph, 38mpg, 0-60mph in 11.7 sec (manual).
Production total: 418,367.

The Vitesse had distinctive alloy wheels and body-coloured mirror housings, as seen on this 1987 model.

The boot lid was enlarged for the 1987 models, to open down to bumper height. This is a 1987 Vanden Plas model, now with 'VP' decals on the rear wings.

With the 216SE came a bright finisher for the bump strip mouldings. Early cars were criticised for awkward boot access: the lid opened above the number-plate.

Late versions of the Vitesse had a different alloy wheel design, plus a 'Vitesse' decal on each rear door.

The 800's lines were clean and chiselled, in the fashion of the mid-1980s. This is an early 820E.

Several police forces took 800s as motorway patrol cars. This is an 827 of Central Scotland Police, with the alloy wheels standard on that model. (PVEC)

The dashboard was even more angular than the exterior, but nonetheless quite stylish.

800 (1986-1998)

The Triumph Acclaim had been a re-badged Honda; the Rover 200 had been a re-worked Honda, but Austin Rover's third collaboration with the Japanese company would be a large car that was designed as a joint venture. There would be distinct Honda and Rover versions of a common design, and each company would be free to develop that design further, as it saw fit. What Rover knew as Project XX and Honda knew as HX was developed from 1982, and the British car was launched as the Rover 800 in 1986, just as Austin Rover became The Rover Group.

All versions were to have front-wheel drive, and the Rover derivatives would have both home-grown engines (a 2.0-litre M-series 16-valve) and a Honda 2.5-litre V6. Styling for Rover was done under Roy Axe, with notably sculpted lines in 1980's vein, while Honda did its own styling. The British car was to be called a Rover 800, in line with the philosophy that saw the SD3 become a Rover 200 in 1984; the Japanese version became a Honda Legend.

All the first 800 models were three-box saloons, badged 820i, 820Si and 825 to reflect their engine sizes. There was also a top model with the V6 engine called the Rover Sterling. For the first two years, Honda would build 800s for Japan in its own factories, while Rover would build UK-market Hondas, but this arrangement was dissolved after Japanese dissatisfaction with British quality control.

Meanwhile, Rover expressed dissatisfaction with the torque delivery of the Honda V6, and the Japanese enlarged it to 2.7 litres, resulting in 827 models from early 1988.

Rover also introduced new Fastback models in 1988, which were not shared with Honda. These stretched the range downwards (with an entry-level 820) and upwards (with a sporty Vitesse, although it had no extra performance). For 1990, new and larger bumpers were added, and at mid-year an 825D diesel model was added, its engine provided by VM in Italy. Then, right at the end of the 1991 model-year, Rover previewed an improved Vitesse with a turbocharged 2.0-litre engine; the 820 Turbo that is often called the 'Tickford Turbo' because the final development was done by Tickford.

The hatchback body, not shared with Honda, was arguably more attractive than the three-box saloon.

Gordon Sked had taken over as design chief at Rover, and his studio produced the face-lifted cars for the 1992 model year. These were developed as the R17 (Fastback) and R18 (Saloon) and brought with them a deliberately more traditional Rover look, with a version of the old Rover grille and more rounded lines. The 2.0-litre cars also had new engines, which were now T16 types with much stronger torque delivery, although the Vitesse retained its V6. Also new in summer 1992, was a svelte two-door 800 Coupé, which had been planned for a long time and arrived rather too late to make the impact it deserved.

The next major changes came in summer 1994, and the most important was that a new Vitesse Sport fulfilled the promise of the 1991 820 Turbo with a turbocharged version of the T16 engine. Then from January 1996, Rover's own 2.5-litre KV6 engine replaced the Honda V6 in top models as part of a series of end-of-life changes to the 800 range. The last 800 was then built in September 1998, and the range was replaced by the new 75.

Between 1987 and 1991, Rover sold the 800 range with V6 engines and Sterling badges in North America, reasoning that the Rover name still had negative associations there after the SD1 had been withdrawn in 1981. Sales were nevertheless disappointing. In Britain, there were also long-wheelbase limousine and six-door derivatives of the 800, and a few hearses as well.

Models: 820, 820E, 820SE, 820i, 820Si,820SLi, 820 Turbo, 825D, 825SD, 825SLD, 825i, 827Si, 827SLi, Vitesse, Vitesse Sport, Sterling, Coupé, Turbo Coupé, Vitesse

The R17 face-lift made the 800 appear more substantial, and the new Rover grille was a big improvement.

The hatchbacks also benefited from the face-lift. This is an 800 Vitesse Sport from 1994.

Face-lift models went to the USA as well. This is an 827 SLi hatchback.

The 800 Coupé was a very attractive derivative, but came too late.

The 1980s was the age of the bodykit, and so one was made available for the 800 in 1987. It was never very popular in the UK.

When the 800 went on sale in the USA, it was badged as a Sterling.

Coupé, Sterling Coupé Sterling (North America): 825S, 825SL, 827SL, 827SLi.

Engines: 1994cc M8 (84.5 x 89mm) DOHC four-cylinder, with 100PS. 1994cc M16 (84.5 x 89mm) DOHC four-cylinder, with 120PS (820E) or 140PS (820i). 1994cc M16 (84.5 x 89mm) DOHC turbocharged four-cylinder, with 180PS (820 Turbo). 1994cc T16 (84.5 x 89mm) DOHC four-cylinder, with 136PS. 1994cc T16 (84.5 x 89mm) DOHC turbocharged four-cylinder, with 180PS (Vitesse) or 200PS (Vitesse Sport). 2494cc Honda C25A (84 x 75mm) 2OHC V6, with 173PS. 2497cc KV6 (80 x 83mm) 4OHC V6, with 175PS. 2498cc VM HR494 (92 x 94mm). OHC four-cylinder diesel, turbocharged and intercooled, with 118PS 2675cc Honda C27A (87 x 75mm) 2OHC V6, with 177PS (later 169PS).

Gearboxes: Five-speed Honda PG1 manual (four-cylinder cars). Five-speed Honda PG2 manual (V6 cars). Four-speed ZF automatic (four-cylinder cars). Four-speed Honda EAT automatic (V6 cars). Four-speed JATCO automatic (KV6 only).

Steering, suspension and brakes: Rack and pinion steering, with standard power assistance. Front suspension with unequal length double wishbones, coil springs with elastomeric spring aids, co-axial telescopic dampers and anti-roll bar. Rear suspension with independent struts, transverse and trailing links, coil spring with elastomeric spring aids, telescopic dampers and anti-roll bar. Disc brakes all round, ventilated on front wheels.

Main dimensions: Length: 4694mm/184.8in. Width: 1730mm/68.1in; 1946mm/76.6in over mirrors. Height: 1398mm/55in. Wheelbase: 2759mm/108.6in. Track: 1492mm/58.7in (front), 1450mm/57.1in (rear).

Performance and fuel consumption: 820E: 119mph, 34mpg, 0-60mph in 10.5 sec (manual). 825D: 118mph, 45mpg, 0-60mph in 10.5 sec. 827Si: 138mph, 29mpg, 0-60mph in 7.6 sec (manual Fastback). Sterling 825: 131mph, 29mpg, 0-60mph in 8.0 sec (automatic). Vitesse Sport: 143mph, 34mpg, 0-60mph in 7.3 sec.

Production totals: 317,126 (including 35,700 Sterling for USA and an estimated 6500 Coupés).

This is a top model 800 Sterling Coupé. By this stage, a third brake light was standard.

Australian 416i (1986-1989)

When Honda ended production of the Quint in Japan, Rover's Australian subsidiary JRA needed

Six-door models were built by MacNeillie. This example was new to a funeral company.

a new medium-sized hatchback to replace their Quintet derivative. Although the Austin Maestro was an obvious contender for the job, import tariffs and exchange rates ruled it out. Instead, JRA chose to take a five-door version of the Honda Integra, built in Japan but badged as a Rover 416i. This car was therefore arguably the first 400-series Rover.

Despite the most un-Rover-like appearance of the car, with its pop-up headlamps, publicity for the new car claimed that "the 416i continues the Rover tradition". Only one model was available as sales began in early 1986, but the 416i was replaced by a two-model range in autumn 1987. The 416i SE was actually less well-equipped than the original car, with painted steel wheels instead of alloys, but the more expensive 416i Vitesse was fully equipped.

A mild face-lift followed, probably during 1988, when the front apron was reshaped, larger front foglights were fitted, and the Vitesse took on a new alloy wheel style. The 416i models remained available into 1989, when Honda brought production of the Integra to an end. JRA considered bringing in the new R8 200 and 400 models, and displayed examples at the Sydney Motor Show in October 1991, but exchange rates once again made the project unviable. So the Australian 416i range was not directly replaced.

Models: 416i, 416i SE, 416i Vitesse.
Engine: 1590cc Honda EP (75 x 90mm) SOHC four-cylinder, with 121bhp.
Gearboxes: Five-speed Honda manual. Four-speed Honda automatic.
Steering, suspension and brakes: Rack and pinion steering with standard power assistance. Independent front suspension with torsion bars, anti-roll bar, and gas telescopic dampers. Rear suspension with coil springs, trailing links, beam axle, Panhard rod, anti-roll bar and gas telescopic dampers. Ventilated disc front brakes and drum rear brakes, with servo assistance standard.
Main dimensions: Length: 4350mm/171.2in. Width: 1665mm/65.5in. Height:1345mm/52.9in. Wheelbase: 2520mm/99.2in. Track: 1420mm/55.9in (front), 1415mm/55.7in (rear).
Performance and fuel consumption: Manual: 121mph, 33mpg, 0-100km/h (62mph) in 10.2 sec.
Production total: No figures available.

Like the Quintet that preceded it in Australia, the 416i was a four-door model with a hatchback.

The 416i was really a rebadged five-door Honda Integra, despite the prominent Rover badge on its nose.

200, second series (1989-1995)

Rover and Honda began work in 1984 on a new compact saloon. Initially known as HY (for the Honda version) and YY (for the Rover one), the joint project became AR8 at Rover in 1985 and then R8 in 1986. For Honda, it would deliver a four-door saloon called the Concerto and would give a valuable new understanding of the European car market. For Rover, it had simply enormous importance: the new platform would provide replacements for the existing 200 series, the Maestro and some models of the Montego, and in due course it would be developed further with niche-market coupé, cabriolet and estate models that were not shared with Honda.

As having separate teams working in different countries had caused problems on the 800-Legend project, this time the Honda and Rover designers worked alongside one another in Japan. So there were far fewer differences between Rover and Honda derivatives than in the 800 and Legend ranges. Rover led the styling, and the Honda car was very similar to it except in cosmetic details. Both had versions of the 1.6-litre four-cylinder Honda engine, while Rover used its own brand-new K-series engine for its 1.4-litre entry models. Later, it would introduce other engines – including Peugeot diesels – to the model mix. Rover agreed to build Concertos at Longbridge alongside its own derivatives, and these Hondas would have the Rover-type MacPherson strut front suspension. However, Japanese-market Concertos built in Japan would have Honda's favoured double-wishbone type.

The Rover 200-series went down very well at its October 1989 launch, even though the Honda had entered production in June 1988. Its styling and interior brought a freshness to the market sector and exuded an air of class which allowed Rover to push prices up. The companion 400-series models followed in April 1990 (and have a separate entry here), and over the next few years the range expanded progressively with new engines and new body styles. The 200-series in particular sold strongly and was a major factor in Rover's survival during the 1990s.

For Rover, the top priority was a five-door hatchback, and this was introduced first. Over the next six years, until the 200 series was replaced during 1995, there was a quite complex evolution of models, and it is easiest to divide the story of the R8 200 into five-door and three-door types. All variants gained the new Rover grille for the 1994 model-year, a year after their 400-series equivalents.

This 216GTi model from 1990 shows the use of dark lower body sides that had been pioneered on the 800 Sterling a few years earlier.

For the 1991 model-year, a body styling kit was available at extra cost. It is fitted here to a 214SLi model.

The first five-door models offered a choice between the 1.4-litre K-series (Si, SLi and GSi models) and 1.6-litre (GSi) Honda engines. A year later the range was expanded with 214S, 216SLi and 216GTi models, the latter with a 130PS twin-cam version of the Honda engine.

The 1992 model-year brought diesel variants, the 218SD (with 1.9-litre Peugeot engine) and 218SLD Turbo (with 1.8-litre turbocharged Peugeot engine). For 1993 the 214S disappeared, but the range was otherwise unchanged. There were then major changes for 1994, as a new entry-level 214i was introduced and the 216 range was slimmed down to just a 216SLi. The performance flagship was a new 220SLi with 2.0-litre M-series engine, and there were two new diesel variants, an entry-level 218D and a mid-range 218SD Turbo.

The five-door range was pruned for 1995. Those remaining were the 214i and 214SLi, which were accompanied by a new mid-range 214SEi. The four diesel models remained available, but all the 216 and 220 models were discontinued for this final production year.

The three-door 200s were always intended to have a more sporting appeal than the five-doors, so there were never any diesels. They were introduced in October 1990 as a 214S, 214Si, 216GTi and 216GTi twin-cam, the former with the SOHC Honda engine and the latter with the DOHC version. For the 1992 model-year a 220GTi was added, then for 1993 the range was cut back to just four models: 214Si, 216GTi, 220GTi and 220GTi Turbo, the latter with the turbocharged T16 engine. For 1994 came a new 214i, the 214Si remained, and there were 220GSi and 220GSi Turbo models; the Honda-engined models were withdrawn. A number of 214 models were given extra equipment and badged as limited-edition Sprint models. There were then no three-door models at all for the final year of R8 200 production.

Models: (Five-door): 214i, 214S, 214Si, 214SEi, 214SLi, 214GSi, 216SLi, 216GSi, 216GTi, 218D, 218SD, 218SD Turbo, 218SLD Turbo, 220SLi. (Three-door): 214i, 214S, 214Si, 216GTi, 216GTi Twin-cam, 220GSi, 220GSi Turbo, 220GTi, 220GTi Turbo.
Engines: 1396cc K-series (75 x 79mm) SOHC four-cylinder, with 75PS. 1396cc K-series (75 x 79mm) DOHC four-cylinder, with 95PS (92PS with cat). 1590cc Honda D16A6 (75 x 90mm) SOHC four-cylinder, with 116PS. 1590cc Honda D16A8 (75 x 90mm) DOHC four-cylinder, with 130PS. 1769cc Peugeot XUD7TE (83 x 88mm) SOHC turbodiesel four-cylinder, with 88PS. 1905cc Peugeot XUD9A (80 x 88mm)

There was a pronounced wedge shape to the lower body, which is exaggerated by this picture of a 1991-model three-door 214Si.

SOHC diesel four-cylinder, with 67PS. 1994cc M-series (84.5 x 89mm) DOHC four-cylinder, with 136PS. 1994cc T-series (84.5 x 89mm) DOHC turbocharged four-cylinder, with 197PS.

Gearboxes: Five-speed Rover-Peugeot R65 manual. Five-speed Honda PG1 manual Four-speed Honda automatic.

Steering, suspension and brakes: Rack and pinion steering; Positive Centre Feel PAS on some models Independent front suspension with MacPherson struts, lower radius arms, longitudinal tie bar and anti-roll bar. Independent rear suspension with twin transverse links, coil springs and telescopic dampers; anti-roll bar on some models. Disc brakes at the front and drum brakes at the rear; some models with ventilated front discs and solid rear discs; ABS optional.

Main dimensions: Length: 4220 mm. Width: 1680mm; 1940mm over mirrors. Height: 1400mm. Wheelbase: 2550mm Track: 1475mm (front), 1470mm (rear).

Performance and fuel consumption: 214i: 100mph, 41mpg, 0-60mph in 12,9 sec 214SEi: 110mph, 40mpg, 0-60mph in 10.7 sec 216 (SOHC): 120mph, 35mpg, 0-60mph in 9.2 sec (manual) 218D: 95mph, 51mpg, 0-60mph in 16.4 sec.

Production totals: 708,069 (including Coupé and Cabriolet).

Five-spoke alloy wheels and a tail spoiler distinguish this twin-cam 216GTi variant.

The high-performance 220GTi model had blacked-out alloy wheels. This is a 1991 car.

Even higher performance could be had from the 220GSi Turbo, although wheelspin was a distinct possibility.

Lattice-work alloy wheels distinguish this 1994-model 2.0-litre-engined 220SLi, a five-door model which also has the latest Rover grille instead of a simple air intake slot.

The five-door 214SEi was a new mid-range model for the cut-back 1995 range.

The Sprint edition was a late model based on the 214Si. This example was sold in the Netherlands.

200 Cabriolet (1992-1999)

The Rover 200 Cabriolet was the first of the R8 derivatives that Rover developed independently of Honda. Work on the car began during 1988 and the project was known as Tracer; after Rover Special Products was formed in 1990, it became that division's responsibility. The Cabriolet was developed around the outer panelwork that had been signed off for the mainstream R8 saloons, and compensation for the absence of a roof was provided by underbody reinforcement and by a sturdy rollover bar.

The 200 Cabriolet was announced at the Geneva Motor Show in March 1992, and went on sale in Britain in April. There were three models, a 214 with Rover's K-series engine, and a Honda-engined 216 with either manual or extra-cost automatic gearbox. All models had split-fold rear seats and a special demister fan for the removable rear window in the convertible roof. This was manually operated as standard, but a power option was available on all models at extra cost. The first cars had a front end with only an air intake slot, but from October 1993 all models carried the latest Rover chrome grille, and by February 1994 an SE trim level had been added. Rover always marketed the 200 Cabriolet as a niche model and as a result the cars remained fairly uncommon.

After the R3 200 became available at the start of 1996, the cars lost their original designations and were simply known as Rover Cabriolets. At the same time, the 1.4-litre models were dropped and a 1.6-litre Rover K-series engine replaced the similarly sized Honda type, while the automatic option now featured a CVT gearbox. The Cabriolet

The first versions of the 200 Cabriolet did not have a Rover grille, but rather a simple slot-type air intake.

also took on an R3-style dashboard and new interior trim.

The 200 Cabriolet went out of production in 1999.

Models: 214, 216 (from 1996, 200 Cabriolet 1.4, 200 Cabriolet 1.6).

Engines: 1396cc K-series (75 x 79mm) DOHC four-cylinder, with 103PS. 1590cc Honda D16A6 (75 x 90mm) SOHC four-cylinder, with 111PS. 1588cc Rover K-series (80 x 79mm) DOHC four-cylinder, with 111PS.

Gearboxes: Five-speed Honda PG1 manual with synchromesh on all forward gears. Four-speed Honda automatic. Four-speed CVT automatic.

Steering, suspension and brakes: Rack and pinion steering with standard power assistance. Independent front suspension with MacPherson struts, coil springs and anti-roll bar Independent trailing-arm rear suspension with twin transverse links and hydraulic telescopic dampers. Ventilated front disc brakes and rear drum brakes with power assistance; rear discs with ABS available at extra cost (1996 on).

Main dimensions: Length: 4218mm (166.1 in) Width: 1679mm (66.1in); 1940mm (76.4in)

over door mirrors Height: 1389mm (54.7 in) Wheelbase: 2550 mm (100.4 in) Track: 1480mm/58.3in (front), 1470mm/57.9mm (rear).

Performance and fuel consumption: 214: 112mph, 38mpg, 0-60mph in 10.5sec. 216 (Honda): 120mph, 33mpg, 0-60mph in 9.0sec. (manual) 117mph, 30mpg, 0-60mph in 10.8sec (automatic). 216 (K-series): 115mph, 40mpg, 0-60mph in 9.7sec (manual). 112mph, 40mpg, 0-60mph in 10.2sec (automatic).

Production totals: Not known (total included in Rover 200, second series).

The 1994 and later models took on the latest chromed grille. This is a 216 model, with alloy wheels.

From March 1996, Cabriolets had an R3-pattern dashboard. Although most seats were grey (including the leather option), this striking two-tone style could be had with Piccadilly cloth upholstery.

Outer panels were from the two-door 200, and a rollover bar provided additional body strength.

The convertible top could be power-operated for extra cost, and was a neat and tight fit.

200 'Tomcat' Coupé (1992-1998)

The plan was always for Rover to make maximum use of the R8 platform, and from 1988 work began on Project Tomcat, a sporty two-door coupé with a wholly Rover-designed superstructure. As signed off for production,

All Coupé models had a small bulge on the bonnet, as seen on this picture of an early 220. The first cars had a simple slot-type front air intake.

The top-model 220 Turbo had appropriate badging at the rear.

Now with a chromed Rover grille on the nose, this is a 1994-model 220 Turbo.

the Tomcat had a curvaceous and attractive two-door body incorporating a sunroof with two lift-out glass panels separated by a removable T-bar. Not one of its exterior panels was shared with the other R8 models. This was the second of the special R8 derivatives, and might have been badged as an MG until the success of the Mazda MX-5 prompted Rover to save the MG name for a new sports roadster – which became the MGF in 1995.

The Rover 200-series Coupé was signed off for production before Rover had decided to standardise a chrome grille on its cars, and so, when introduced at the Paris Salon in October 1992, it had only an air intake slot in the nose, even though new models of the R8 introduced at the same time had the new grille. There were four models, called 216, 216 Automatic, 220 and 220 Turbo. Honda provided the engine and gearboxes for the 216 models, while the other two had the Rover T-series engine and PG1 five-speed gearbox.

The 220 Turbo boasted a turbocharged engine with 200PS and a top speed of 150mph, and to tame its power it had a Torsen differential, which was also available as an option on the naturally-aspirated 220 Coupé. For some export territories, the 216 models had a more powerful twin-cam Honda engine. Both 2.0-litre cars had a boot-mounted spoiler.

Ash Grey cloth seats were standard, with leather bolsters on the Turbo and an all-leather option. Burr walnut contributed a Rover ambience, and all models had a practical split-fold rear seat. The cars were generally well received, although the Torsen differential and wider tyres were not the whole answer to the 220 Turbo's torque steer.

Autumn 1993 brought the first changes, when all models gained a chromed Rover grille and the 1.6-litre models switched from steel disc wheels to seven-spoke alloys. But there were cost savings, too, as the dashboard lighting dimmer and ignition keylock light were deleted, and the amount of leather in the interior was reduced. In 1993-1994, Rover sponsored the Dunlop Rover Tomcat Race Series, providing a total of 36 specially-prepared 220 Turbo models for this one-make series that was held at venues in the UK and Europe. After 1994, the company withdrew its sponsorship and the series evolved into the Stafford Landrover Super Coupé Cup, in which the Rovers continued to race for a time.

During the first half of 1995, Rover introduced a 216 SE Coupé, which was primarily intended to help clear stocks of the 216 model before its replacement was introduced in the autumn. The 216 SE was distinguished by a rear spoiler (from the 220 Turbo) and front fog lamps.

The 1996 model range was completely revised, and now consisted of just three models, all with new names. The Rover Coupé 1.6 could be had in manual or automatic form, and now had Rover's own K-series engine. Above it came the Rover Coupé 1.8 VVC, with the variable-valve 1.8-litre K-series also used in the MGF. Though quick enough, this car was not a match for the now deleted 220 Turbo.

Both cars had a new dashboard similar to that of the latest R3 200-series cars, made possible because Coupés and R3 shared the same bulkhead structure. Cloth seats were standard on the 1.6, now in lighter Piccadilly Grey with either red or grey centres, and the

car had steel wheels with plastic trims, but could be ordered with alloys as an option. The 1.8 VVC had alloys as standard, while its cloth seats came with leather-trimmed bolsters. Both could have Smokestone leather at extra cost.

In this guise, the Tomcat Coupé remained in production until 1998, but Rover chose not to replace it.

Models: 216, 216 Automatic, 216SE, 220, 220 Turbo; Coupé 1.6, Coupé 1.8VVC.
Engines: 1590cc Honda D16A6 (75 x 90mm) SOHC four-cylinder, with 111PS. 1590cc Honda D16A8 (75 x 90mm) DOHC four-cylinder, with 122PS (export only). 1997cc Rover T16 (84.45 x 89mm) DOHC four-cylinder, with 136PS. 1997cc Rover T16 (84.45 x 89mm) DOHC turbocharged four-cylinder, with 200PS. 1589cc Rover K-series (80 x 79mm) DOHC four-cylinder, with 111PS. 1796cc Rover K-series (80mm x 89.3mm) DOHC four-cylinder, with 145PS.
Gearboxes: Five-speed Honda manual with synchromesh on all forward gears Five-speed PG1 manual with synchromesh on all forward gears Four-speed Honda automatic.
Steering, suspension and brakes: Rack and pinion steering with standard power assistance. Independent front suspension with MacPherson struts, coil springs and anti-roll bar. Independent trailing-arm rear suspension with twin transverse links and hydraulic telescopic dampers. Disc front brakes and drum rear brakes with power assistance (1.6-litre models); ventilated front discs and solid rear discs with ABS (1.8-litre and 2.0-litre models).
Main dimensions: Length: 4270mm (168.1in) Width: 1679mm (66.1in); 1940mm (76.4in) over door mirrors Height: 1369mm (53.9in) Wheelbase: 2550mm (100.4in) Track: 1480mm/58.3in (front), 1470mm/57.9mm (rear)
Performance and fuel consumption: 216: 120mph, 31mpg, 0-60mph in 9.5sec 216 Automatic: 118mph, 31mpg, 0-60mph in 11.2sec 220: 127mph, 36 mpg, 0-60mph in 8.2sec 220 Turbo: 150mph, 35mpg, 0-60mph in 6.2sec 1.6 Coupé: 1.8 VVC Coupé:
Production totals: Not known (total included in Rover 200, second series).

Bright colours added to the appeal of the coupés, but the later 1.8 VVC flagship model seen here was not as quick as the legendary 220 Turbo.

47

400, first series (1990-1995)

Right from the start of the R8 project, Rover planned to make maximum possible use of the new platform that they were developing jointly with Honda. So in addition to the multiple models that became the second-generation Rover 200, the company developed a three-box saloon that was brought to market in April 1990 as the Rover 400, to compete in the small medium class.

The 400 shared the chiselled lines of the 200 range, but Roy Axe's rear-end redesign of the glasshouse recalled the design of the Montego; Honda adopted it for the three-box version of its Concerto that was developed from the same joint project. Rover made extensive use of zinc-

The entry-level model in 1990 was the 414Si, with star-pattern plastic wheel trims.

Recognition features of the 416GTi were the alloy wheels and dark grey lower body panels.

All the first 400-series cars had a simple air intake slot on the nose. This was a mid-range model for 1991.

coated steel to improve the cars' resistance to corrosion, and built the 400s at Longbridge alongside their 200 siblings.

The first cars came as 414 models with the 1.4-litre K-series engine, or as 416 models with Honda engines. There were Si and SLi trim levels for the 414, which could be had with catalytic converters at extra cost, while the better-equipped 416GSi had Honda's 114bhp Honda 1.6-litre SOHC engine. The flagship model was a 416GTi 16-valve, with the 128bhp twin-cam version of the Honda engine, and this combined a luxurious leather-upholstered cabin with sporty performance. ABS was optional on all variants, on the 416s automatic was optional and air conditioning standard, and the 416GTi had Positive Centre Feel PAS, which was optional elsewhere.

This range was mildly tweaked in November 1990, when lower-specification 416Si and 416SLi models were added and a body styling kit became available as an option. Then, from March 1991, the 400 range gained diesel options, as did the 200. The 418SLD and 418GSD both had a Peugeot 88PS turbocharged 1.8-litre engine, driving through the Honda-designed PG1 gearbox. Then, from October 1992, all 400s gained the new corporate Rover grille and monochromatic rear light lenses. Two new 2.0-litre engines delivered six new models. The 136PS T-series was for the 420SLi and 420GSi, plus Executive and Sport derivatives of the latter model. The second engine was a 200PS turbocharged T-series, which created the limited-availability 420GSi Sport Turbo.

This view of a 1990 414SLi shows how the rear of the glasshouse resembled that of the Montego.

Range realignments in November 1993 parallelled those for the 200 models. All the GS models were absorbed into the SL range, while the GTi and Sports models were redesignated GS. The diesel range was expanded, too, with a 418SD Turbo and a new entry-level 418SD, with a naturally-aspirated 1.9-litre Peugeot diesel engine. Final changes were made in March 1994, when a driver's side airbag became standard on SL models and above.

The 400 range had been joined by a Tourer estate derivative in 1993 (see separate entry), which remained in production after the saloon models were replaced in summer 1995 by the second-generation 400 series.

Models: 414Si, 414SLi, 416Si, 416SLi, 416GSi, 416GTi, 418SD, 418SD Turbo, 418SLD, 418GSD, 420SLi, 420GSi, 420GSi Executive, 420 GSi Sport, 420GSi Sport Turbo.

Engines: 1396cc K-series (75 x 79mm) DOHC four-cylinder, with 95PS (92PS with cat) 1590cc Honda D16A6 (75 x 90mm) SOHC four-cylinder, with 116PS 1590cc Honda D16A8 (75 x 90mm) DOHC four-cylinder, with 128PS (122PS with automatic gearbox) 1769cc Peugeot XUD7TE (83 x 88mm) SOHC turbodiesel four-cylinder, with 88PS 1905cc Peugeot XUD9A (80 x 88mm) SOHC diesel four-cylinder, with 67PS 1994cc T-series (84.5 x 89mm) DOHC four-cylinder, with 136PS 1994cc T-series (84.5 x 89mm) DOHC turbocharged four-cylinder, with 197PS.

Gearboxes: Five-speed Rover-Peugeot R65 manual. Five-speed Honda PG1 manual Four-speed Honda automatic.

Steering, suspension and brakes: Rack and pinion steering; Positive Centre Feel PAS on some models Independent front suspension with MacPherson struts, lower radius arms, longitudinal tie bar and anti-roll bar. Independent rear member with double wishbones and compensating trailing arm; separate spring-and-damper units; anti-roll bar on some models. Disc brakes at the front and drum brakes at the rear; some models with ventilated front discs and solid rear discs; ABS optional.

Main dimensions: Length: 4365mm. Width: 1680mm; 1940mm over mirrors. Height: 1400mm. Wheelbase: 2550mm. Track: 1475mm (front), 1470mm (rear).

Performance and fuel consumption: 414: 106mph, 41mpg, 0-60mph in 11.1sec. 416 SOHC: 120mph, 35mpg, 0-60mph in 9.2sec (10.8sec with automatic gearbox). 416 DOHC: 124mph, 34mpg, 0-60mph in 8.6sec (10.3sec with automatic gearbox). 418 (1.8): 106mph, 46mpg, 0-60mph in 11.8sec. 418 (1.9): 96mph, 47mpg, 0-60mph in 16.0sec. 420: 126mph, 36mpg, 0-60mph in 8.1sec. 420 Turbo: 146mph, 35mpg, 0-60mph in 6.4sec.

Production totals: 245,630 (including Tourer)

400 Tourer (1994-1998)

Rover's third special variant of the R8 platform was a compact four-door estate car. Intended as a 'lifestyle' model rather than a big load carrier, it was given the name of Tourer and was aligned with the more expensive 400 range rather than the 200 series. Work on what was called Project Tex had started in 1988 and continued under Rover Special Products in 1990, but the 400 Tourer was not introduced until March 1994, at the Geneva Motor Show.

The overall design was very well resolved, although the Tourer was never intended to be a big load-carrier.

The 400 Tourer was designed to look smart and sophisticated, and was always more prestigious (and more expensive) than its obvious rivals.

Rover initially promoted it as the flagship of the 400 range, and focused publicity on its sharp styling, luxurious interior furnishings, and sporting nature. Certainly, there were no 'entry-level' models, and the range consisted of 1.6-litre and 2.0-litre petrol models, with a 1.8-litre turbocharged diesel option as the main concession to practicality. The 1.6-litre engine was the only one available with an automatic gearbox option.

However, after the second-generation Rover 400 was introduced in 1995, the 400 branding was removed from the older model, which became a plain Rover Tourer. A 1.8 VVC model was promised to replace the 2.0-litre petrol models from summer 1996, but production was delayed and in practice only a handful were ever made. By October 1997, the only models left in production were 1.6 and 1.6SE types.

The 400 Tourer sold well, even though Rover had always considered it a niche model, and it remained in production into 1998, nearly three years after its 400 saloon siblings had been replaced by a new model.

Models: 416SLi, 418SLD Turbo, 420GSi (1.6SLi, 1.8SLD and 2.0GSi from mid-1995).
Engines: 1590cc Honda D16A6 (75 x 90mm) SOHC four-cylinder, with 111PS. 1769cc Peugeot XUD7TE (83 x 88mm) SOHC turbodiesel four-cylinder, with 88PS. 1796cc K-series (80 x 89.3mm) VVC four-cylinder, with 145PS 1994cc T-series (84.5 x 89mm) DOHC four-cylinder, with 136PS.
Gearboxes: Five-speed Honda PG1 manual. Four-speed Honda automatic.
Steering, suspension and brakes: Rack and pinion steering with Positive Centre Feel PAS as standard. Independent front suspension with MacPherson struts, lower radius arms, longitudinal tie bar and anti-roll bar Independent rear member with double wishbones and compensating trailing arm; separate spring-and-damper units; anti-roll bar on some models Ventilated disc brakes at the front and drum brakes at the rear.
Main dimensions: Length: 4370 mm/172in. Width: 1680mm/66.1in; 1940mm/76.4in over mirrors. Height: 1400mm/55.1in Wheelbase:

2550mm/100.4in Track: 1480mm (front), 1475mm (rear).
Performance and fuel consumption: 416: 115mph, 31mpg, 0-62mph in 10.5sec (manual) 112mph, 30mpg, 0-62mph in 12.3sec (automatic). 418: 105mph, 46mpg, 0-62mph in 13.3sec 420: 122mph, 38mpg, 0-62mph in 9.2sec.
Production totals: Figures included in overall 400 production totals.

Rover Metro & 100 (1990-1997)

Rover had planned to replace the Austin Metro with a new supermini developed as the AR6, but during 1987 this was cancelled on cost grounds. In its place came the R6 project, for a 'Mk 3' revision of the Metro. It was this car that became the Rover Metro on its launch in May 1990; in some European countries it was called the Rover 100 series from the start.

The Rover Metro looked much like the old Metro, despite a new front end design and improved interior. It was also a much better car to drive, thanks to a new version of its Hydragas suspension with interconnection between front and rear, and to new K-series engines. There were 1.1-litre and 1.4-litre options, with a more powerful 16-valve 1.4 engine with single-point injection in the three-door GTi. For the moment, there were no K-series models with automatic gearboxes, and so the old Metro automatic remained available with its A-series engine. However, sales were already beginning to slide, and the Rover Metro probably did no more than slow the decline.

From June 1991, a 500-strong special edition of the 1.4 GTi (with part-leather upholstery)

This early 1.4GS model is the five-door Rover Metro, with its new front end design featuring the Rover Viking ship shield badge.

featured a more powerful engine with multi-point injection. Also new were a sporty 1.4 GTa, with more power than the other eight-valve 1.4-litre models, and Advantage and Sport 1.1-litre limited editions.

The anticipated automatic derivatives arrived in May 1992, with a CVT gearbox made by Volvo in Belgium, allied to the 1.4-litre engine. At the same time, a 1.4-litre Peugeot engine delivered the first-ever diesel Metros. A month later, entry-level models gave way to Metro Quest and Quest Plus models: a strategy that suggested these were exclusive special editions. The 1.4-litre GTi now switched permanently from a single-point injection engine to the more powerful multi-point injection type.

Autumn 1992 then brought the promise of a cabriolet derivative, developed as a niche model by Rover Special Products, but sales did not begin until early 1994. Perhaps no more than 200 were ever made, all probably with the 1.4-litre petrol engine, as the high price deterred buyers. From December 1992, all Metro petrol engines had petrol injection.

There were also several special editions of the Rover Metro. These were the Impression (February 1993), Rio and Rio Grande (August 1993), Tahiti, Tahiti Special, Nightfire and Nightfire Special (December 1993), Casino and Casino Royale (April 1994), Rio and Rio Grande (second version, June 1994), and GTa SE (June 1994).

The 'Mk4' Metro was developed as a substantial face-lift of the Rover Metro and was launched in December 1994. The 1.6-litre models disappeared, and the diesel was up-engined to 1.5 litres. These cars were now called Rover 100 models in all markets, and had a new Rover

grille, though without the chrome of other Rovers of the time. There were also changes to the bumpers, sills, headlamps and boot handle, but even though the availability of leather upholstery in the top model 114GSi brought a more credible degree of Rover character, the car did not have enough new features to be very convincing.

Three-door and five-door models (as they were called) were available from the beginning, but the cabriolet derivative was delayed until June 1995. Once again, only 1.4-litre versions of this were sold in the UK. It was also in June 1995 that Rover replaced its entry-level 111i and 111Si models by named variants with a special edition flavour, called the Kensington and Kensington SE. The strategy was continued in April 1996 when the entry-level models (now including a diesel) became the Knightsbridge and Knightsbridge SE; and its final iteration in June 1997 brought the Ascot and Ascot SE models.

The Rover 100 cannot have been expected to stay in production for much longer (the basic Metro design was already 17 years old), but its end was hastened by a disastrous result in the new EuroNCAP crash-safety test. As word spread, so sales dried up, and Rover decided to cut its losses and stop production in December 1997.

The Rover 100 was not directly replaced, although the newer and smarter R3 200-series cars were already catering for many potential customers.

Models: (Rover Metro): 1.1C, 1.1L, 1.1S, 1.4CD, 1.4LD, 1.4Li (auto), 1.4Si, 1.4SL, 1.4GS, 1.4GSi, 1.4 GTa, GTi (Rover 100): 111i, 111Si, 111SLi, 114SLi, 114GTa (three-door only), 114GSi (five-door only), 115SD, 115SLD.

All Metros were hatchbacks, and this rear view shows an early three-door 1.1L model.

The Rover Metro became a police car, too. This example belonged to London's Metropolitan Police.

Engines: 1120cc K-series (64.6 x 76.2mm) SOHC four-cylinder, with 61PS. 1360cc Peugeot TUD3 (75 x 77mm) SOHC diesel, with 52PS. 1396cc K-series (75 x 79mm) SOHC four-cylinder, with 76PS. 1396cc K-series (75 x 79mm) DOHC four-cylinder, with 96PS, later 103PS. 1527cc Peugeot TUD5 (77 x 82mm) SOHC diesel, with 57PS.

The Cabriolet was never very numerous. The 100-series versions, like this late 114 model, had grey convertible tops; the Rover Metro versions had black tops.

From late 1994, the Metro became a Rover 100-series in all its markets, and took on a new front end with a subdued version of the latest Rover grille. This is a mid-range model, with the S or SL specification.

The GTa SE was a sporty special edition from summer 1994.

Gearboxes: Five-speed Peugeot R65 manual CVT automatic optional on 1.4 models.

Steering, suspension and brakes: Rack and pinion steering with standard power assistance. Hydragas gas springs, interconnected front to rear. Front suspension with MacPherson struts incorporating coil springs, anti-roll bar and hydraulic telescopic dampers. H-frame torsion beam rear suspension, with coil springs and hydraulic telescopic dampers. Disc front brakes and drum rear brakes with standard power assistance.

Main dimensions: Length: 138.6in. Width: 61.5in; 69.9in over mirrors. Height: 54.2in Wheelbase: 89.4in Track: 51.2in (front), 51in (rear).

Performance and fuel consumption: 1.1i/111i 97mph, 46mpg, 0-62mph in 13.7sec. 1.4i/114i 105mph, 42mpg, 0-62mph in 10.5sec. 114i CVT 100mph, 41mpg, 0-62mph in 11.1sec. 1.4i Spi 113mph, 42mpg, 0-62mph in 9.6sec. 1.4i Mpi 116mph, 42mpg, 0-62mph in 8.6sec. 1.4 D 88mph, 56mpg, 0-62mph in 16.8sec. 115D 96mph, 50mpg, 0-62mph in 15.3sec.

Production totals: R6 Metro: 389,224 Rover 100: 170,262.

Rover 600 (1993-1998)

Back in 1984, Rover had planned a new medium-sized saloon on a shortened 800 platform as an eventual replacement for the Austin Montego, and some work had been done on this concept, which was to deliver a four-door saloon (AR16) and a five-door hatchback (AR17). However, a re-think shortly after the formation of the Rover Group in 1986 led to the cancellation of these programmes.

When the matter of a replacement for the Montego re-surfaced in 1989, the choice fell on a 'Roverised' Honda design. The Japanese company did have a car of the right size in the pipeline, but it already had a very clear idea of the way it wanted to go and did not want any Rover input into the design. So the deal signed in June 1989 allowed Rover to redevelop the forthcoming Honda Accord, but only after the Japanese had finished their work on it.

In practice, the Accord design team would incorporate many lessons learned from Rover into their new car, and the Rover engineers worked alongside them in Japan in order to get their version of the Accord ready in time for its planned launch. However, this was very much 'arm's length' co-operation; Rover were given the completed Japanese designs on which they could then base their own car. Rover initially knew the new car by the code-name of Synchro, but before long that changed into SK1 (for versions that would use Honda engines) and SK2 (for those with Rover engines). The SK codes reflected the co-operation between the two companies: S was for Rover's George Simpson, and K was for Honda's Nobuhiko Kawamoto.

With this project came a welcome departure from the square-rigged styling that had characterised the designs of the 1980s. Richard Woolley joined the Synchro team after working on the R8, and he drew up a much more rounded style for the new car, incorporating the traditional-style Rover grille that was characteristic of the company's latest cars. It was a huge success in customer clinics, and this persuaded the Rover management to move the new car up-market and to make it more than a replacement for the Montego; instead, it became a 'compact executive' class competitor, priced just below premium mid-size saloons like the Mercedes-Benz 190, BMW 3-Series and Audi A4.

The new car was called the Rover 600 when it was launched in April 1993, fitting into the Rover line-up between the existing 400 and 800 models. All models were built at Cowley, while Honda built the related Accord at its Swindon plant. All the first variants had Honda engines, initially 2.0-litres and then adding 2.3-litres in late 1993. The next addition was the high-performance 620ti in July 1994, with Rover's 200PS turbocharged T16 engine, 16-inch alloy wheels, re-worked suspension, a Torsen differential and half-leather seats. Diesel models joined the range in January 1995, becoming the first cars with Rover's new L-series engine.

When the 600 was launched, Rover's press pictures were still resolutely black and white. This is a very early 620Si model, with the standard steel disc wheels and plastic trims.

A subtle spoiler-like lip gave definition to the boot lid, which carried the model designation on early cars. This is a 620 SLDi, again with plastic wheel trims on steel disc wheels. Sill panels were black on the earlier cars.

Then in February 1996 the base model was re-engineered with a 1.8-litre Honda engine.

There were of course various trim levels over the years, entry-level 'i' or 'Di' being followed by Si or SDi (with split rear seats), SLi or SLDi (with wood on the doors and electric rear windows), and then GSi or GSDi (with leather and air conditioning) as the top option. The 620ti was the only one with that designation, and the 623iS added a sporty appearance to the biggest-engined model. Derivative badges were abandoned in 1996, in favour of a universal "600" on the boot lid. At the same time, all models gained a third brake light, some interior revisions, and equipment upgrades. There was then a minor face-lift in 1997, characterised by a lower ride height and body-colour sills, side rubbing strips, door handles and mirror bodies.

Late models included iL (Luxury) and iS (Sporty) derivatives of the lower-specification variants.

The 600 went down very well in the beginning, and sold particularly strongly in the fleet market, where its restricted rear legroom was not a major deterrent. However, its life was inevitably shortened by the BMW take-over in 1994. BMW did not want internal competition for their own 3-Series (the hot-rod 620ti being a particular offender in that respect), and nor did they want to continue paying royalties to Honda for the 600 range. So production was brought to an end in 1999, and the 600's place in the Rover hierarchy was absorbed by the new 75.

Models: 618, 618iL, 618iS, 620, 620i, 620iL, 620iS, 620Si, 620SLi, 620ti, 620Di, 620SDi,

The 620SLDi was always an attractive purchase. This 1996 model belonged to Rover's press fleet.

The high-performance 620ti was a real wolf in sheep's clothing. It was almost indistinguishable from a lesser 600, and in this picture even the alloy wheels are almost invisible.

Twin tailpipes, six-spoke alloy wheels and, of course, a 620ti badge reveal exactly what this car is.

620SLDi, 620GSDi, 620GSi, 623, 623iS, 623SLi, 623GSi.
Engines: 618: 1849cc Honda F18A (85 x 81.5mm) SOHC four-cylinder, with 115PS. 620i: 1997cc Honda F20Z1 (85 x 88mm) SOHC four-cylinder, with 115PS. 620ti: 1997cc Rover T16 (84.45 x 89mm) DOHC turbocharged four-cylinder, with 200PS. 620 (diesel): 1994cc Rover L-series (84.5 x 88.9mm) SOHC four-cylinder intercooled turbodiesel, with 105PS. 620 (others): 1997cc Honda F20Z1 (85 x 88mm) SOHC four-cylinder, with 131PS. 623: 2259cc Honda H23A3 (87 x 95mm) DOHC four-cylinder, with 158PS.
Gearboxes: Five-speed Honda PG1 manual. Four-speed Honda automatic standard on 623GSi and optional on others.
Steering, suspension and brakes: Rack and pinion steering with standard power assistance

Independent front suspension with double wishbones, coil springs, anti-roll bar and hydraulic telescopic dampers. Independent rear suspension with double wishbones, coil springs, anti-roll bar and hydraulic telescopic dampers. Disc brakes all round, ventilated at the front and solid at the rear; power assistance and ABS standard (except on 618i)
Main dimensions: Length: 4645mm. Width: 1715mm. Height: 1380mm Wheelbase: 2720mm. Track: 1475mm (front), 1480mm (rear).
Performance and fuel consumption: 618i: 121mph, 33mpg, 0-60mph in 10.5sec (manual) or 13.0sec (automatic). 620i: 123mph, 35mpg, 0-60mph in 10.1sec. 620Si, SLi & GSi: 125mph, 33mpg, 0-60mph in 9.5sec (manual) or 11.2sec (automatic). 620SDi & SLDi 115mph, 50mpg, 0-60mph in 10.8sec. 620ti: 143mph, 30mpg, 0-60mph in 7.0sec.
Production total: 272,512.

Rover believed the 620ti might appeal as a high-speed police pursuit car, and prepared this example as a demonstrator for UK police forces.

From April 1997, the sills, bump strips, door handles and mirror bodies were all painted to match the body. This is a 1.8-litre model, which, by that stage, was the entry-level 600.

Among the last 600s were models called the iS and IL, which added extras like alloy wheels to models with an otherwise fairly low specification.

400, second series (1995-1999)

Just one joint project with Honda was in progress when BMW moved in, and this was the new 400, scheduled to replace the R8 model with that name in 1995. Work had begun in 1991, with Rover's initial styling proposals being produced under the code-name of Theta. However, the programme was soon re-baptised as HH-H (the Honda version) and HH-R (the Rover version).

As with the 600-Concerto programme, Honda had already decided on what it wanted for their new car – to be badged as the Civic – and this left little room for Rover to manoeuvre. The British company's task was made doubly difficult by the fact that Honda's starting point was a singularly unattractive creation for the Japanese home market that bore the name of Domani.

Honda wanted only a five-door hatchback for the Civic, but Rover decided to create a four-door saloon as well, and started work on that in July 1993. It tweaked the suspension to give its versions of the car a softer ride, and it gave the 400 a more British character by specifying primarily Rover engines for it. These were the K-series in 1.4-litre and 1.6-litre sizes, the T-series in 2-litre form, and the new 2-litre L-series diesel. This would be the first appearance of the 1.6-litre K-series, but it gave way to the Honda 1.6-litre engine in models with an automatic gearbox.

Rover's five-doors appeared first, with either 1.4-litre or 1.6-litre engines; only the 416SLi could be purchased as an automatic. The promised 2.0-litre petrol and 2.0-litre diesel models became available in March 1996, the diesels being available in both 86PS (420D,

The second-generation 400-series could look quite dumpy from some angles, and publicity pictures like this one were deliberately taken from low down. This is an early five-door model, with the amber direction indicator lenses.

This five-door has been heavily accessorised, with a spoiler, roof rack, towbar and other items. A rear wash-wipe was standard on five-door versions of the 400.

420SD) and 105PS intercooled (420SDi, 420SLDi and 420GSDi) forms. From March 1997, a new 'S' trim level was introduced, delivering 414S, 416S, and 420DS Turbo models.

The four-door saloon, meanwhile, was promised from the April 1995 launch, announced at the Frankfurt Show in September 1995 and went on sale in March 1996. From the start it had 1.6-litre, 2.0-litre and diesel engine options. It was 175mm longer than the hatchback model, the extra length being at the rear. Saloons also had a black feature band on their bumpers, and smoked indicator lenses from the beginning. There was never a 1.4-litre saloon – the four-door range initially being perceived as slightly more up-market than the hatchback (although prices would later be harmonised). The first cars shared designations with the five-door types. One additional model, the 416S, arrived in spring 1997, and from about the same time, air conditioning became standard and there were new seat trims as well as other equipment upgrades. A 420Di Turbo was also added to the range.

From May 1998, four- and five-door models followed the same evolution. May brought 416LS models of each, with leather trim as standard, plus some further equipment

upgrades. Then from April 1999 there was a series of changes designed to get the last of the original cars through the showrooms before the new 45 models arrived in the autumn. As a first stage, all models were renamed 400SEi, 400iL and 400iS (with all engine options), and then from June the final examples were badged as 400iE, 400iXL and 400 Executive.

One special edition of the four-door was promised but never delivered. Probably encouraged by the Rover Group's then-owners BMW, a 425 V6 model was developed for the Frankfurt Motor Show in September 1997, and appeared later that month at the London Motor Show as well. It had Rover's latest 2.5-litre KV6 engine, as introduced in the 800 range earlier in the year, and was promised as a summer 1998 limited edition of 500 cars. However, teething troubles with the KV6 engine and the cost of the forthcoming upgrade to a Rover 45 probably explain why nothing more was heard about the car, which would certainly have improved the rather staid image that the second-generation 400-series always had.

Models: (Five-door): 414, 414i, 414Si, 416i, 416Si, 416SLi, 420D, 420Di Turbo, 420SD, 420SDi, 420SLDi, 420GSDi, 420i, 420Si, 420SLi,

This is the four-door saloon, with longer rear end and no rear wash-wipe. The rear lights were deliberately different from those on five-door 400s, and the bumpers have a black band as well.

420GSi, 400SEi, 400iL, 400iS (Four-door): 416i, 416Si, 416SLi, 420D, 420Di Turbo, 420SD, 420SDi, 420SLDi, 420GSDi, 420i, 420SLi, 420GSi, 400SEi, 400iL, 400iS.

Engines: 1396cc K-series (75 x 79mm) DOHC four-cylinder, with 103PS. 1589cc K-series (80 x 79mm) OOHC four-cylinder, with 111PS. 1590cc Honda D16A6 (75 x 90mm) SOHC four-cylinder, with 113PS. 1994cc T-series (84.5 x 89mm) DOHC four-cylinder, with 136PS. 1994cc L-series (84.5 x 89mm) turbodiesel four-cylinder, with 86PS 1994cc L-series (84.5 x 89mm) intercooled turbodiesel four-cylinder, with 105PS.

Gearboxes: Five-speed Rover-Peugeot R65 manual. Five-speed Honda PG1 manual. Four-speed Honda automatic.

Steering, suspension and brakes:
Rack and pinion steering, with standard power assistance. Independent front suspension with double wishbones, coil springs, gas filled telescopic dampers and anti-roll bar. Multi-link rear suspension incorporating wishbone, coil springs and gas-filled telescopic dampers.

Disc brakes at the front, solid on 1.4 and ventilated on 1.6 and 2.0; drum brakes at the rear; ABS standard on 2.0-litre petrol models and optional on others; rear discs standard with ABS.

Main dimensions: Length: 4316 mm (five-door); 4491mm (four-door). Width: 1695mm; 1908mm over mirrors. Height: 1385mm. Wheelbase: 2622mm. Track: 1475mm (front), 1465mm (rear).

Performance and fuel consumption:
414: 115mph, 41mpg, 0-60mph in 11.0sec. 416 manual: 118mph, 40mpg, 0-60mph in 10.0sec. 416 auto 118mph, 34mpg, 0-60mph in 12.0sec. 420 diesel: 105mph, 58mpg, 0-60mph in 13.0sec. 420 int dsl: 115mph, 59mpg, 0-60mph in 10.4sec. 420 petrol: 124mph, 37mpg, 0-60mph in 9.0sec.

Production totals: 469,781 (also quoted as 469,885).

The 416LS was introduced in 1998 as a special edition and is seen here in four-door saloon guise. The longer tail of the saloon made the styling much better balanced than that of the five-door hatchback.

Introduced early in 1997, this is a five-door 416S model.

The black bumper trims mark this as a four-door saloon, in this case fitted with alloy wheels and dating from 1997.

The 425 V6 was displayed at motor shows but unfortunately did not enter production as promised.

200, third series (1995-1999)

Rover Group's plans to replace the Metro went through several stages. The re-skinned, re-engined R6 that entered production as the Rover Metro and became the Rover 100 was just the first. Roy Axe's team In the Design Studio developed their ideas further to produce R6X but costs put paid to that. The next proposal, in late 1990, was called SK3, and would have been an adapted Honda model, but that too was cancelled on cost grounds.

Meanwhile, more modern Metro rivals were tending to be larger cars, and so the engineers began to think of using a cut-down R8 platform for a Metro replacement. Early work suggested that boot space would be poor, so the rear end of the Maestro platform with its H-frame torsion beam suspension was grafted on and by May 1991 the project had become the R3, with a somewhat restrictive development budget of £200 million.

The design team settled on a shape by Dave Saddington, which could be adapted easily into both three-door and five-door designs and had a very attractive coupé-like look. Development was put on hold for six months during 1992 while the company focussed on other priorities, but a target launch date of autumn 1995 was set. Then during 1994, the Marketing Department reached the conclusion that R3 could be positioned more up-market than the Metro and so, instead of becoming a new Rover 100, the car was developed as a new Rover 200.

The third-generation 200 was launched at the London Motor Show in October 1995, and sales began at the start of 1996. The petrol engines were all K-series types, creating 214i, 214Si and 216Si models, plus a 216SLi available only as a five-door. There were two versions of the L-series diesel as well, creating 220D, 220 SD and 220SDi models, the latter two only sold as five-doors. Gearboxes were the Peugeot-Rover R65 manual from the R8 with a four-speed CVT option on 1.6-litre models. A three-door 1.8-litre model with the VVC engine from the MGF was also announced as a 200vi, but

actual availability was delayed until January 1997 because of high demand for that engine in the MG; even then, five-door models were further delayed until July.

The R3 was a delightful and competitive entry to the market, available in a range of

Top of the range at launch was the 216SLi five-door model, with alloy wheels as standard.

Although the 200vi was announced in 1995, in practice none were available until 1997. This 1.8-litre performance model was initially available only with the three-door body.

The R3 body was curvaceously attractive, and clever use of a 'spoiler' over the rear window helped make it look longer, too. There were no model badges at the rear.

bright colours to help it appeal to younger buyers, and between 1996 and 1998 was Britain's seventh best-selling car. There were regular range realignments from 1997, as specifications and options were improved, and there were new engines, too: a 1.8-litre without VVC from July 1997, and a 1.1-litre from January 1998. From February 1998, all R3 models came with green-tinted Optikool glass as standard, and front seats were improved. Then, from February 1998, there was the Rover 200 BRM, previewed at the Frankfurt and London Motor Shows a year earlier, and intended as a sporty limited edition based on the 200vi.

Staffordshire Police was a big fleet customer, taking 125 five-door diesels from 1997.

The range realignments between 1997 and 1999 brought far more new designations than there is room to list here. By summer 1999 as production drew to an end, the R3 range in the UK was quite bewildering. It consisted of 211SE, 211iE, 214SE, 214 iE (with both 8v and 16v engines), 214iL, 214iS, 216iL, 216iS, 220SE, 220iE (with either 86PS or 105PS), 220iL, 220iS, 200vi and 200 BRM. Broadly speaking, E stood for Equipment, S for Sport and L for Luxury.

Models: 211i, 211iE, 211SE, 214, 214i, 214iE, 214iL, 214iS, 214S, 214Si, 214SE, 216iL,

The iS models introduced in summer 1997 had alloy wheels as standard.

This March 1997 picture shows a three-door S model with standard alloy wheels and a five-door 214 with steel wheels and plastic trims.

216iS, 216Si, 216SLi, 218iS, 200 BRM, 200vi, 220D, 220SD, 220DS Turbo, 220SDi, 220SE, 220iE, 220iL, 220iS.
Engines: 1120cc K-series (64.6 x 76.2mm) SOHC four-cylinder, with 60PS. 1396cc K-series (75 x 79mm) SOHC four-cylinder, with 75PS. 1396cc K-series (75 x 79mm) DOHC four-

For 1998, the entry-level model was a 211i, seen here as a five-door.

The Si trim level was designed to emphasise the sporty side of the R3. This is a 1998-model three-door.

This late-model 200 in five-door SE trim was pictured with a number-plate intended to encourage sales from August 1999. In practice, the cars would be replaced by Rover 25 models just a few months later.

cylinder, with 103PS. 1589cc K-series (80 x 79mm) DOHC four-cylinder, with 111PS. 1796cc K-series (80 x 89.3mm) DOHC four-cylinder, with 120PS. 1796cc K-series (80 x 89.3mm) DOHC VVC four-cylinder, with 145PS. 1998cc L-series (84.5 x 88.9mm) SOHC four-cylinder turbocharged diesel with 86PS. 1998cc L-series (84.5 x 88.9mm) SOHC four-cylinder turbocharged and intercooled diesel, with 105PS.
Gearboxes: Five-speed Rover-Peugeot R65 manual. Four-speed CVT automatic optional with 1.6-litre engine.
Steering, suspension and brakes: Rack-and-pinion steering with standard power assistance. Independent front suspension with MacPherson struts, coil springs, anti-roll bar and hydraulic telescopic dampers. H-frame torsion beam rear suspension, with coil springs and hydraulic telescopic dampers. Disc front brakes and drum rear brakes, with standard servo assistance; disc rear brakes on 200vi.
Main dimensions: Length: 3973 mm. Width: 1688mm. Height: 1419mm. Wheelbase: 2502mm Track:1472mm (front), 1466mm (rear).
Performance and fuel consumption: 214i: 103mph, 44mpg, 0-60mph in 12.5sec. 214Si: 115mph, 43mpg, 0-60mph in 10.2sec. 216Si & SLi: 118mph, 43mpg, 0-60mph, in 9.3sec. 216 CVT: 115mph, 41mpg, 0-60mph in 9.8sec. 200vi: 127mph, 43mpg, 0-60mph in 7.5sec. 220D & SD: 105mph, 51mpg, 0-60mph in 12.0sec. 220SDi: 115mph, 50mpg, 0-60mph in 9.8sec.
Production totals: 470,449, including Rover BRM (also quoted as 470,503) 200BRM: 1145 (795 for the UK and 350 for export).

Publicity for the 200 BRM linked the car to the 1965 Rover-BRM gas turbine racer and the BRM Formula 1 cars of the 1960s.

75 (1998-2005)

By the time of the BMW takeover in early 1994, Rover had embarked on a series of new designs that were of its own creation, even though some Honda mechanical components might have been incorporated. The aim was to focus on traditional Rover qualities in both styling and mechanical areas, and to deliver premium products that could be priced accordingly. The only one of these projects which had become a full engineering project was for an eventual replacement for the Rover 800.

BMW looked hard at this and for a time there was a plan to build the car on a BMW 5-Series rear-wheel-drive platform. Then during 1994 the focus switched to a Rover-designed front-wheel-drive platform, the project became R40, and the car was re-positioned between the existing 600 and 800 models so that it would not clash with BMW's own models. The main legacy of BMW's involvement was a version of its Z-axle suspension at the rear. Gordon Sked's designers chose a visual theme originally proposed by Richard Woolley for a new 600, and this was continued under Geoff Upex when he became Rovers' design and concept director in March 1995.

The new car was called a Rover 75, deliberately recalling the 'classic' period of the Rover P4, but also indicating that the car was aimed mid-way between the existing 600 and 800 models. At launch in October 1998 it was widely acclaimed as an exceptionally attractive design, and the first customer cars were delivered in June 1999.

The petrol engines were all Rover's own K-series types, in 1.8-litre four-cylinder and 2.0 and 2.5 V6 sizes. BMW supplied the diesel engine, which was its admired 2-litre M47 type, re-worked for a transverse installation as the R47. Plans for further derivatives – sporty saloons (which eventually wore MG badges) and Tourers (estates) – were already in hand when the Rover Group was sold to Phoenix in May 2000. Rover 75 production was transferred from Cowley to Longbridge in August.

The new Tourer became available in May 2001 after an optimistic early announcement in June 2000, and was again a most attractive and well-

A key feature of the new 75's style was the design of the paired headlamps. The overall shape was curvaceous and contemporary.

The Tourer was a most attractive design, done with input from Ian Callum at TWR, who would later become Jaguar's chief designer.

The 1999 and 2000 model 75s had sills and lower bumpers painted black (not visible here) and a lozenge-shaped badge on each front door.

Roof bars were standard on the Tourer, and that object on the rear roof housed aerials for the radio and (when fitted) satellite navigation system.

resolved design. MG variants of the 75 (badged as ZT types) went on sale in September 2001, and at the same time Rover announced a Monogram custom-finishing programme which actually began the following March.

Autumn 2002 then brought new engines – a turbocharged 1.8-litre (which replaced the 2.0 V6) and a more powerful version of the existing diesel, which went on sale alongside the original. A Rover 75 finished under the Monogram programme was made the celebratory Five Millionth Rover in July 2003. But the major news for the 75 family that year was the introduction of a new V8 model, initially available only with MG badges. The engine came from Ford in America and was the one used in the Mustang; installing it had involved re-engineering the 75 for rear-wheel drive – although of course other models retained their front-wheel drive. When the Rover version of the V8 arrived in March 2004, it could be had only with an automatic gearbox and high levels of trim and equipment.

Meanwhile, the 75 had also been made available as a long-wheelbase limousine from

2002, initially with the Vanden Plas name, and as a six-door limousine conversion from 2003. Some were even built as hearses. For the mainstream models, however, MG Rover attempted to maintain the freshness of the design with a face-lift, overseen by chief designer Peter Stevens and introduced in January 2004. Done on a tight budget, this was more successful on the MG derivatives than on the Rovers.

The Rover 75 remained available with 1.8, 1.8 turbo, 2.5 V6, CDT and CDTi engines until

Initially known as the Rover Vanden Plas, this was the long-wheelbase derivative of the 75.

The Monogram custom-finishing service brought special-effect paints and two-tone schemes like the one seen on this Tourer.

Few six-door limousines were built, and all were conversions by MacNeillie. This one was used by Exeter City Council.

The interior was deliberately intended to recall the opulence of older Rovers. This one has the optional wood-and-leather steering wheel, plus a sat-nav system.

production was halted in April 2005 when MG Rover went under. The car's design was sold to China, where it reappeared for a time in modified form as the Roewe 750 and the MG 7.

Models: 1.8, 1.8 Turbo, 2.0, 2.5, V8. Trim levels; Classic, Classic SE, Club, Club SE, Contemporary, Contemporary SE, Connoisseur, Connoisseur SE, Vanden Plas.
Engines: 1796cc K-series (80 x 89.3mm) DOHC four-cylinder, with 120PS. 1796cc K-series (80 x 89.3mm) DOHC turbocharged four-cylinder, with 150PS. 1951cc BMW R47 (84 x 88mm) DOHC turbocharged and intercooled four-cylinder, with

116PS. 1951cc BMW R47 (84 x 88mm) DOHC turbocharged and intercooled four-cylinder, with 131PS. 1991cc KV6 (80 x 66mm) 4OHC V6-cylinder, with 160PS. 2497cc KV6 (84 x 88mm) 4OHC V6-cylinder, with 177PS 4601cc Ford (90.2 x 90mm) DOHC V8-cylinder, with 260PS.
Gearboxes: Five-speed Getrag manual. Five-speed JATCO automatic.
Steering, suspension and brakes:
Rack-and-pinion steering with standard power assistance. Independent front suspension with MacPherson struts, coil springs, anti-roll bar and gas-filled telescopic dampers. Independent rear suspension with Z-axle, coil springs and gas-filled telescopic dampers. Disc brakes all round, ventilated on front wheels; standard servo assistance and ABS.
Main dimensions: Length: 4745mm/186.8in (Saloon) 4790mm/188.6in (Tourer). Width: 1970mm/77.5in over door mirrors. Height: 1427mm/56.2in 1480mm/58.3in over Tourer roof rails. Wheelbase: 2745mm/108in. Track: 1505mm/59.2in (front and rear).
Performance and fuel consumption:
1.8: 121mph, 36mpg, 0-60mph in 10.9sec. (manual) 1.8 turbo: 130mph, 35mpg, 0-60mph in 9.1sec. (Saloon) 126mph, 35mpg, 0-60mph in

The 2004 face-lift brought new front and rear details, and most notably an enlarged grille and a different headlight treatment.

At the rear, the 2004 models lost the bright strips from the bumpers and gained a new '75' badge below the number-plate.

The V8-engined models were all 'face-lift' types. Just visible here is the bright-metal V8 badge on the front wing.

First seen in November 2004, the Rover 75 Coupé was a concept that lifted spirits at the company, but time was running out and it did not enter production.

9.1sec (Tourer). 2.0: 127mph, 25mpg, 0-60mph in 10.8sec (automatic). 2.5: 134mph, 24mpg, 0-60mph in 8.9sec (automatic). 2.0 CDT: 120mph, 46mpg, 0-60mph in 11.0sec (manual). 2.0 CDTi: 120mph, 48mpg, 0-60mph in 11.0sec (manual). V8: 151mph, 21mpg, 0-60mph in 6.8sec (Saloon). 147mph, 21mpg, 0-60mph in 7.0sec (Tourer).
Production total: 211,175.

Rover 25 (1999-2005)

The mid-life overhaul for the R3 200-series Rovers became a thorough re-working as the cars were given the new four-lamp front end of the Rover 75, revised engines, new interiors, a more sporty chassis tune, and a number of other improvements derived from the 75. Developed as Project Jewel, the face-lifted cars were also re-named as Rover 25 models when they were introduced in November 1999. As before, both three- and five-door bodies were available.

There were six engines at launch, mostly

The 75-style headlamps gave new character to the front end of the 25. This is a 2003-model five-door 1.6iL, with Stepspeed CVT gearbox.

Reprofiled bumpers and a chrome strip above the number-plate were the main changes at the rear. This is an early three-door model.

revised versions of those seen in the last 200s. Manual gearboxes were standard, and the six-speed CVT automatic option on the 1.8-litre models now had the Steptronic manual over-ride control system developed by BMW. The seven levels of trim were based on the formula used successfully for the 75, and there was a selection of new alloy wheels.

Promised 1.1-litre and 1.6-litre Steptronic models were delayed while Rover became MG Rover, and became available in early 2001. Plans for an MG derivative of the 25 were announced during 2001 but availability of the MG ZR was not until early 2002; the 1.8-litre and VVC models of the Rover 25 were then dropped to protect MG sales. The CVT gearbox was now available only with the 1.6-litre engine, and its control system was rebranded as Stepspeed.

Meanwhile, there had been added-value Impression and Impression S special edition packages in January 2001; Olympic Impression and Olympic Impression S packages in October that year; and Spirit and Spirit S packages in July 2002. A 25 was among the cars that introduced the Monogram custom-finishing service at the Frankfurt Show in September 2001, although actual availability was not until around March 2002 – and Monogram 25s would be rare. From February 2002 there was a 25 CDV (Car Derived Van) with either the 1.4-litre 8-valve petrol engine or the 2.0-litre diesel, and this became another rarity.

In September 2003, a Getrag IB5 manual gearbox replaced the earlier R65 type in the 1.4-litre and 1.6-litre models, and the final changes came in April 2004, when the 25 range was face-lifted by Rover's chief designer Peter

Destined to be rare, this was the 2003-model Rover CDV.

Stevens. The obvious differences lay in the headlamps (actually unchanged, but behind new shaped glass covers) and the rear panel. This limited-budget face-lift carried the 25 through to the collapse of MG Rover in April 2005.

Models: 1.1, 1.4 8v, 1.4 16v, 1.6, 1.8, VVC, 2.0 Diesel; 1.4 CDV, 2.0 Diesel CDV.
Engines: 1120cc K-series (64.6 x 76.2mm) SOHC four-cylinder, with 60PS. 1396cc K-series (75 x 79mm) SOHC four-cylinder, with 84PS. 1396cc K-series (75 x 79mm) DOHC four-cylinder, with 103PS. 1589cc K-series (80 x 79mm) DOHC four-cylinder, with 109PS. 1796cc K-series (80 x 89.3mm) DOHC four-cylinder, with 117PS. 1796cc K-series (80 x 89.3mm) DOHC VVC four-cylinder, with 145PS. 1994cc L-series (84.5 x 88.9mm) SOHC four-cylinder turbocharged diesel, with 100PS.
Gearboxes: Five-speed Rover-Peugeot R65 manual. Five-speed Getrag IB5 manual. Six-speed CVT Steptronic automatic optional with 1.6-litre and (early) 1.8-litre engines.
Steering, suspension and brakes:
Rack-and-pinion steering with standard power assistance. Independent front suspension with MacPherson struts, coil springs, anti-roll bar and hydraulic telescopic dampers. H-frame torsion beam rear suspension, with coil springs and hydraulic telescopic dampers. Disc front brakes and drum rear brakes, with standard servo assistance; disc rear brakes on VVC.
Main dimensions: Length: 3990 mm. Width: 1690mm. Height: 1420mm. Wheelbase: 2500mm. Track: 1470mm (front and rear).
Performance and fuel consumption: 1.1: 100mph, 41mpg, 0-60mph in 13.5sec. 1.4 8v: 105mph, 42mpg, 0-60mph in 11.8sec. 1.4

16v: 112mph, 42mpg, 0-60mph in 10.2sec. 1.6: 115mph, 42mpg, 0-60mph in 9.5sec. 1.8: 115mph, 34mpg, 0-60mph in 9.5sec. VVC: 124mph, 37mpg, 0-60mph in 7.8sec. Diesel: 113mph, 55mpg, 0-60mph in 9.9sec.
Production total: 249,000 approx (cars). 1000 approx (Commerce vans).

Rover 45 (1999-2005)

The Rover 45 was created out of the second-generation Rover 400 and was really a face-lifted version of that car that was given a separate identity. The main influence on it was the Rover 75, and the new 45 took on a version of that car's four-headlamp front end, with a raised bonnet line and deeper grille than on the last of the 400s.

The 1.4-litre and 1.6-litre K-series engines, and the 2.0-litre L-series diesel, were carried over to the 45 and were supplemented by the new 1.8-litre K-series and 2.0-litre KV6. Both four-door saloon and five-door hatchback bodies remained available, although only the five-door could be had with the 1.4-litre engine. Steptronic control was used for both automatic gearboxes,

The April 2004 face-lift brought more angular lines to the front end, plus a new satin-finish '25' badge on each front door.

The changes at the rear helped the car to look lower. This is a 2004 three-door 25.

Very rare indeed, this is the CDV version of the face-lifted car.

a five-speed JATCO that was standard with the V6 and a six-speed CVT type optional with the 1.8. There were several interior changes from the 400s, and there were five different trim levels, as on the 75.

The Rover 45 had been on sale for just under nine months when the Rover Group was sold and became MG Rover, and plans for new derivatives of the range were already in place. Among these new derivatives were to be MG-badged variants, which were introduced in 2001 (and are not described here). They became MG ZS types.

Over the next two years, Rover introduced several special editions and equipment enhancements to keep the 45 range fresh.

January 2001 brought the Impression (five-door) and Impression S (five-door and saloon); October 2001 had the Olympic Impression (five-door) and Olympic Impression S (five-door and saloon); and in July 2002 came the Spirit (five-door) and Spirit S (five-door and saloon). LPG conversions were introduced for the 1.8-litre models in July 2002, and for the 1.4-litre and 1.8-litre types in January 2003. Meanwhile, there were range-wide equipment and cosmetic changes from October 2002, and that December

the L-series diesel engine was uprated to 113PS.

By this stage, the 45 was past its planned sell-by date. Under BMW ownership, Rover would have replaced it in 2002 or 2003 with the new R30 model, but the sale of Rover to the Phoenix Consortium had put paid to that. The April 2004 face-lift then, by Rover's chief designer Peter Stevens, was to some extent an act of desperation carried out on a minimal budget, delivering a reasonably attractive new front end but a very plain-looking rear. It was in this face-lifted guise that the 45 struggled on for another year, until MG Rover collapsed and production ended.

Models: 1.4 (five-door only), 1.6, 1.8. 2.0 diesel, 2.0 V6. Engines: 1396cc K-series (75 x 79mm) DOHC four-cylinder, with 103PS. 1589cc K-series (80 x 79mm) DOHC four-cylinder, with 111PS. 1796cc K-series (80 x 89.3mm) DOHC four-cylinder, with 117PS. 1991cc KV6 (80 x 66mm) V6, with 150PS. 1994cc L-series (84.5 x 89mm) intercooled turbodiesel four-cylinder, with 101PS; 113PS from December 2002.

Gearboxes: Five-speed JATCO automatic (with

The 75-derived front end sat less well on the 45 than on the smaller 25, the excessively thick grille frame being very noticeable.

The bright-finish alloy wheels certainly enhance the appearance on this special-edition Impression saloon model.

This early 2.0 V6 model has the top level of trim, known as Connoisseur.

The boot of the 45 saloon was not a great aesthetic success, and looked bulbous. This is an Olympic Impression special edition model.

Steptronic). Five-speed Honda PG1 manual. Six-speed CVT with Steptronic.

Steering, suspension and brakes: Rack and pinion steering, with standard power assistance. Independent front suspension with double wishbones, coil springs, gas filled telescopic dampers and anti-roll bar. Multi-link rear suspension incorporating wishbone, coil springs and gas-filled telescopic dampers. Disc brakes at the front and drum brakes at the rear; ABS standard.

Main dimensions: Length: 4363 mm (five door); 4517mm (four-door). Width: 1910mm over mirrors. Height: 1395mm. Wheelbase: 2620mm. Track: 1480mm (front), 1470mm (rear).

Performance and fuel consumption: 1.4: 115mph, 40mpg, 0-60mph in 11.2sec. 1.6: 118mph, 40mpg, 0-60mph in 10.3sec. 1.8: 121mph, 39mpg, 0-60mph in 9.3sec. (manual) 118mph, 32mpg, 0-60mph in 10.3sec. (automatic) 2.0 V6: 127mph, 30mpg, 0-60mph in 9.5sec. 2.0 diesel: 115mph, 52mpg, 0-60mph in 10.6sec (101PS). 118mph, 50mpg, 0-60mph in 9.8sec (113PS).

Production totals: 156,000 approximately.

The April 2004 face-lift was quite successful at the front end, especially the new grille.

However, the rear end changes were not a success on the saloon, where the boot bustle looked more bulbous than ever.

Interestingly, the 2004 face-lift worked much better on the shorter tail of the 45 five-door.

There was never a Tourer version of the 45, but Rover did experiment by adding 45 front end panels and other details to a Honda estate. The car remained unique and, after a collision, was rebuilt with 'face-lift' 45 front end panels.

Streetwise (2003-2005)

Realistically, the Streetwise was a somewhat desperate attempt by MG Rover to get more life out of an existing platform that was, by 2003, already eight years old. The aim was to attract younger drivers: 25- to 35-year-olds who wanted "a street credible car that complements their modern active lifestyle and makes a statement about their personality," according to the launch press release.

To that end, the Rover 25 was turned into an 'urban on-roader,' with raised suspension, rugged-looking bumpers, standard roof bars and a lot of accessories. There was a precedent of sorts, too: Renault had tried something similar with its surprisingly successful Mégane Scenic RX4 model.

At the September 2003 launch, there were three basic Streetwise models, with 1.4 SOHC and 1.4 DOHC K-series engines, plus a 2.0-litre L-series diesel. 1.6-litre and 1.8-litre K-series engines followed later, the 1.8-litre coming only with a Stepspeed CVT gearbox. Only the

1.4 SOHC and 2.0 diesel engines could be had with basic trim, which featured steel wheels; all engines were available with the S trim level, and all except the 1.4 SOHC with top-level SE trim.

The standard four-seat interior featured a full-length centre console, but a five-seat model with shorter console was available. Switchgear and instruments were subtly different from their Rover 25 equivalents, and a Trafficmaster congestion-warning system was standard. Basic models were

Roof bars, a raised ride height, and chunky grey front and rear aprons distinguished the Streetwise from its parent Rover 25. Entry-level models had steel wheels instead of these 16-inch alloys.

The Streetwise name was carried on the side cladding rather than on traditional badges.

The extra plastic cladding supposedly made the Streetwise well suited to the bustle of a city environment.

complemented by S and SE trim levels. The Streetwise went out of production in 2005 when MG Rover collapsed, but the basic design was sold to Nanjing in China, where it reappeared in 2008 with MG3 SW badges.

Models: 1.4, 1.4S. 1.4SE. 1.6S, 1.6SE, 1.8S. 1.8SE, 2.0 Diesel S, 2.0 Diesel SE.
Engines: 1396cc K-series (75 x 79mm) SOHC four-cylinder, with 84PS. 1396cc K-series (75 x 79mm) DOHC four-cylinder, with 103PS. 1589cc K-series (80 x 79mm) DOHC four-cylinder, with 111PS. 1796cc K-series (80 x 89.3mm) DOHC four-cylinder, with 117PS. 1998cc Rover L-series (84.5 x 88.9mm) SOHC four-cylinder diesel with turbocharger and intercooler, and 101PS.
Gearboxes: Five-speed Getrag IB5 manual with 1.4 and 1.6-litre engines. Five-speed Honda PG1 with diesel engine. Four-speed CVT automatic standard with 1.8-litre engine.
Steering, suspension and brakes: Rack and pinion steering with standard power assistance. Front suspension with MacPherson struts incorporating coil springs, anti-roll bar and hydraulic telescopic dampers. H-frame torsion beam rear suspension, with coil springs and hydraulic telescopic dampers. Disc front brakes and drum rear brakes with standard power assistance.
Main dimensions: Length: 3980mm. Width: 1736mm (1946mm over door mirrors). Height: 1495mm. Wheelbase: 2505mm. Track: 1473mm (front), 1466mm (rear).
Performance and fuel consumption: 1.4 SOHC 102mph, 38mpg, 0-60mph in 11.8sec. 1.4

There was an extensive accessories range for the Streetwise. This one has 17-inch alloy wheels and side runners, while the front has a nudge bar and headlamp guards.

DOHC 108mph, 38mpg, 0-60mph in 10.2sec.
1.6 118mph, 37mpg, 0-60mph in 9.3sec. 1.8
115mph, 34mpg, 0-60mph in 9.9sec. 2.0 diesel
113mph, 47mpg, 0-60mph in 9.9sec.
Production totals: 11,000 approximately.

CityRover (2003-2005)

The CityRover was immediately recognisable, but UK sales never really got off the ground. This early example is a low-specification model with steel wheels sporting plastic trim covers.

In the early 2000s, MG Rover needed a small economy car in its range, to sell to customers who might once have bought a Metro or Rover 100. However, the company's lack of investment capital ruled out the possibility of developing a new model, and the solution chosen was to buy one in from outside and to re-badge it as a Rover.

The choice fell on the Tata Indica, a front-wheel-drive supermini which was a best-seller in India, where it was made. Introduced in 1998, the Indica was at the time the most modern passenger car ever built in India, featuring a body designed with assistance from IDEA in the UK and an engine based on a Peugeot design and called the 475DL. Manufacturing costs in India were very low, with the result that the car could be sold in the UK at a substantial profit. Stories from the period suggested that the £6495 showroom price of the entry-level Rover version was more than twice its purchase cost from Tata. Part of the deal appears to have been that MG Rover would assist in the marketing of Tata pick-ups in the UK, but this arrangement was never very productive.

The tall and narrow proportions of the CityRover were well suited to its city-car role, but presented some challenges to the stylists.

The Rover version of the car was given the project code of RD10 and was introduced in autumn 2003 as the Rover CityRover. All examples were built at Tata's plant in Pune, and incorporated special Rover elements: a Rover grille, different bumpers, different suspension settings and 14-inch wheels. The only powertrain option was a 1.4-litre four-cylinder petrol engine with five-speed manual gearbox. However, there were four different trim levels, called Solo, Sprite, Select and Style.

The dashboard of the CityRover was very much in tune with the economy-car theme, and the interior had little that could be considered recognisably Rover.

The first CityRovers were poorly received by the motoring media, who criticised their build quality, performance and handling. Sales were disappointing, too, and so Rover improved equipment levels for the 2005 model-year,

A number of CityRovers remained unsold when MG Rover went under. This one, with the alloy wheels and additional grilles of the high-specification cars, was not registered until 2006.

also reducing prices by £900 (nearly 14%) in December 2004. This was not enough to revitalise sales, and the CityRover remained a slow seller until MG Rover collapsed in April 2005. The last few examples were sold at discounted prices, but many took some time to find buyers.

The Tata Indica, meanwhile, remained a best seller in its native country and was updated with a second-generation model in 2008. Its successors were still strong sellers at the time of writing.

Models: 1.4.
Engine: 1405cc (75 x 79.5mm) SOHC four-cylinder, with 86PS.
Gearbox: Five-speed manual with synchromesh on all forward gears.
Steering, suspension and brakes:
Rack and pinion steering with standard power assistance. Independent front suspension with McPherson struts and anti-roll bar Independent rear suspension with coil springs, semi-trailing arms and hydraulic telescopic dampers. Ventilated front disc brakes and drum rear brakes, with standard servo assistance and ABS.
Main dimensions: Length: 3703mm/145.8in. Width: 1620mm/63.8in; 1924mm/75.7in over mirrors. Height: 1500mm/59.1in. Wheelbase: 2400mm/94.5in. Track: 54.3in/1380mm (front), 54.1in/1374mm (rear).
Performance and fuel consumption: 100mph, 37mpg; 0-60 in 11.9sec.
Production totals: 10,000 (approximately).

The non-Rovers (1986-2000)

When the Rover Group was formed in 1986 out of what had once been British Leyland, it inherited cars of diverse origins. Some of these were, and always had been, Rovers. Production of the SD1 was just coming to an end, and it was about to be replaced by the 800 Series; both of these were Rovers. Still in production was the SD3 or Rover 200 Series, which had also always been a Rover (despite its Honda origins).

However, there were also four ranges of cars that had not started life as Rovers. These were the Mini, the Metro, the Maestro and the Montego. All of them would continue in production under the Rover Group, but they would not take on Rover badges in most of the countries where they were sold. The Rover Group's Managing Director Kevin Howe referred to them as Non-Rovers, which was as apt a description as any. The Maestro and the Montego lived and died as Non-Rovers, going out of production in 1992, and the Mini retained its own distinctive branding and survived as a Non-Rover until 2000. However, the Metro gained Rover badges in 1990 after four years as a Non-Rover. All four models are discussed briefly here, but the Rover-badged versions of the Metro have a more comprehensive treatment elsewhere in the book.

Mini, 1987-2000

Introduced in 1959 as an Austin Seven and a Morris Mini Minor, the Mini was one of the great success stories of the British motor industry. Primarily a two-door saloon, it also spawned estate, van and pick-up models, and even an open recreational variant called the Moke. It was in Mk II form with 848cc and 998cc engine options when British Leyland was formed, and then became a Mk III in 1969 and was renamed the Leyland Mini. At this stage, a 1275GT model replaced the Mini Cooper as the performance

By the time of the Rover Group, the Mini was on 12-inch wheels rather than its original 10-inch size, but was still recognisably the car that had been introduced in 1959. Dating from 30 years after that, this is a Mini City model.

derivative, with the revised front end of the new Clubman model.

Only minor changes to the Mini range were made during the 1970s, and from 1975 a 1098cc engine became standard on most models. Then during 1980 the 1098cc and 1275cc engines disappeared and a 998cc A-Plus type (developed for the Metro that was introduced that year) became standard. This smaller engine helped protect Metro sales, and the size of the Mini range was reduced for the same reason. Estate production ended in 1982.

Sales of the Mini dipped during the 1980s, but to keep the model fresh there was a multiplicity of special editions that traded on the car's fashionable appeal. Then Rover Group revived the Mini Cooper in 1990, adding fuel injection to its 1275cc engine a year later. This seemed to give the marque a new lease of life, and by 1994 the Mini had become the best-selling Rover Group model in many export countries, selling even more in Japan than it did in Britain. All models had 1275cc injection engines from 1992, and a year later a Mini Cabriolet was added to the range. Boosted by regular special editions, sales remained strong until the car was finally taken out of production in October 2000, giving way to a new Mini designed under the BMW regime. Although often referred to as a Rover Mini, the car did not wear Rover badges for most countries where it was sold.

Metro, 1987-1990

The Metro was introduced in 1980 as the Austin Mini Metro, a front-wheel-drive two-door supermini with transversely mounted engine. It was intended to replace the Mini, but the Mini continued to sell alongside it, and so the Metro found its niche as a slightly larger, better-equipped model in the modern hatchback idiom. Between 1980 and 1984, it was British Leyland's best-selling model and regularly figured in the top ten best-selling cars in Britain. Engines were 1.0-litre (998cc) and 1.3-litre (1275cc) A-plus types, and there were MG and Vanden Plas derivatives, as well as a van that initially wore Morris badges.

A Mk 2 Metro range, now including both four-door and two-door models, was introduced in

The Metro was the car that had to save British Leyland – and did – after 1980. This is a two-door model from the late 1980s, by which time it was wearing the 'cross' type of grille badge associated with the Rover Group.

This was the 'cross' pattern of grille badge. It always carried the model name rather than the maker's name, and in this case, was on a Mini.

1984, and this was still in production when the Rover Group was formed in 1986. Following the success of the strategy with the Mini, the Metro was then made available in multiple special editions. In 1987 it lost its Austin branding and became a plain Metro, until a further face-lifted model introduced in 1990 saw it renamed as a Rover Metro. All Metro variants were built at Longbridge.

Maestro, 1987-1992

Launched as an Austin Maestro in 1983, this was one of British Leyland's new mid-range models; the other was the closely related Montego. It had 1.3-litre and 1.6-litre engine options, with front-wheel drive and a four-door body with a hatchback. MG and van versions became available, and the top model was badged as an Austin Maestro Vanden Plas. Key new features were electronic engine management systems, a bonded windscreen and a 'voice synthesis' (speaking) dashboard that was not liked and was soon discontinued. All Maestros were built at Cowley.

From 1987, the Austin name disappeared and the model became a plain Maestro. That year, the vans gained a diesel option (the noisy Perkins Prima engine), and this became available in saloons as well from 1990. The range was cut back in 1989 as its R8 (Rover 200) replacement came on stream, and the last Maestros were built in the UK in 1992.

Then, in 1997, a store of unused CKD components intended for overseas assembly was rediscovered. It was sold off to a UK company which assembled them and sold them as new cars up to 2001. The Maestro tooling, meanwhile, was sold to China for further use there.

The Maestro always kept its Austin Rover chevron grille badge, even under the Rover Group. This late 1980s example is a Maestro Special.

Montego, 1987-1995

The Montego was the three-box saloon version of the design that had delivered the Maestro, and was introduced with Austin badges in 1984. It had a longer wheelbase than the Maestro, but shared most of that car's mechanical elements. Despite some deliberate styling differences, the two models also shared well over half of their body panels.

When the Rover Group was formed in 1986, the Austin Montego was available with 1.3-litre A-Plus, 1.6-litre S-series, and 2.0-litre O-series engines, as a four-door saloon and also as a much-liked estate with the two larger engines. There were high-performance MG variants and well-appointed Vanden Plas variants as well. Like the Maestro, the Montego lost its Austin badges in 1987. A mild face-lift then distinguished the Mk II models introduced under the Rover Group in 1988, which also gained a 2.0-litre diesel engine option and a more performance-oriented model with the injected 2.0-litre engine from the MG models. The 1.3 models were dropped in 1989, and saloon production then continued until 1993, giving way to the new Rover 600. The estates continued into 1995.

Under the Rover Group, the Montego was known simply by that name, but Rover badges were added for some export territories, of which France and Italy were examples.

The Montego was the three-box relative of the Maestro. This example has the 'cross' style of grille badge used in Rover Group days.

The estate was a popular variant of the Montego. This is a 1987 left-hand-drive model for Europe, with the 2.0-litre engine.

Gas turbines

Rover engineers worked on jet aero engine development during the 1939-1945 war. Although they handed the work over to Rolls-Royce in 1943, Maurice Wilks saw the engine's potential for road use. In 1945, he began work on a gas turbine engine for cars, using the jet exhaust stream to drive a power turbine that in turn drove the wheels.

The first Rover gas turbine car was completed in 1950, and gained the registration JET 1. It was based on a Rover 75 saloon, converted to open two-door configuration with the engine mounted amidships. The car was subsequently modified with a more streamlined front end and in June 1952 set a world record of just under 152mph on the Jabbeke highway in Belgium.

Rover then put a gas turbine engine into a P4 saloon in 1952, but the exhaust run from front to rear caused problems and so T2 was rebuilt as T2A with a rear-mounted gas turbine in 1954. It was not a great success.

The third gas turbine car was designed by Spen King and became T3 in 1956. This was a purpose-built coupé, with rear engine and four-wheel drive. Encouraged, the Rover engineers next planned a gas turbine option for the P6 saloon, and one prototype of that car was built up as T4 in 1961. However, anticipated high production

JET 1 still survives, and belongs to the Science Museum collection.

T3 was an attractive little coupé, finished in light blue.

costs terminated the gas turbine car programme, although Solihull did supply standalone gas turbine engines for a variety of purposes. Rover had one more crack at the idea, when they fitted a gas turbine engine into a BRM racing chassis and gave it a new body in 1963. Rebodied after an accident, the Rover-BRM ran successfully at Le Mans in 1965 (although it was not competing in the event).

The shape of T4 is quite obviously that of the Rover 2000 (P6), and the car was built from a prototype P6 base unit.

The Rover-BRM, seen here with its second body, ran successfully at Le Mans.
(WikiMedia Commons/David Merrett)

How to power tune Rover V8 engines

Covers all Rover 3.5, 3.9, 4.0 & 4.6 litre engines from 1967 to date. Get maximum road or track performance & reliability for minimum money. The author is an engineer with much professional experience of building race engines. Suitable for the enthusiast as well as the more experienced mechanic. All information is based on practical experience.

ISBN 978-1-787111-76-9

Rover P4

The definitive history of the dignified Rover P4 from 1949 until 1964, which includes Marauder and jet-powered, experimental cars. Affectionately known as the 'auntie' Rovers, these models have become much-loved classics and represent the epitome of Britishness.

ISBN 978-1-845849-58-0

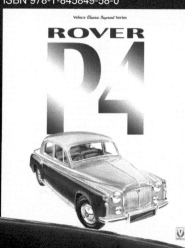

www.veloce.co.uk

The Essential Buyer's Guide™ series ...

Index

Alvis   25, 27
Austin inheritance   7
Austin Rover   6
Axe, Roy   37, 48, 59

Bache, David   17, 20, 23, 25, 27, 28, 31
Bashford, Gordon   14, 20, 23, 26, 27
BMW   8, 34, 53, 54
British Aerospace   9
Buick   23, 24, 26

Chapron   21, 25
China   9, 64, 69
Crayford   26

Exner, Virgil   13

FLM Panelcraft   22, 25, 26

General Motors   23, 24, 29
Graber   15, 21, 25

Honda   39-42, 44, 46, 48, 52, 53, 57, 59, 62, 71
Honda alliance   7

King, Spen   23, 26, 30, 74

Land Rover   8
Lyons, Sir William   27, 30

Marauder   19
MG Rover   9
Model P   14
Monogram programme   63

Peugeot   49, 50, 51, 61, 66
Phoenix Group   9
Pinin Farina   17

Rover Group   7, 9
Rover Special Products   44, 49, 51
Rover-British Leyland   6, 7

Sked, Gordon   38, 62
Sterling   36
Stevens, Peter   63, 66, 67
Swaine, Jack   11, 14, 23

Tata   70, 71
Turnbull, George   27

Weslake, Harry   22
Wilks, Maurice   13, 14, 15, 16, 74
Wilks, Peter   23
Woolley, Richard   53, 62

Zagato   25, 27

Visit Veloce on the web:

www.velocebooks.com / www.veloce.co.uk

Details of all current books ● New book news ● Special offers